To:

From:

Date:

when holidays hurt

Finding Hidden Hope Amid Pain and Loss

BO STERN

THOMAS NELSON
Since 1798

NASHVILLE   MEXICO CITY   RIO DE JANEIRO

To my ALS Wives Support Group: women who love fiercely, live sacrificially, and never stop believing for a world without wheelchairs, feeding tubes, and breathing machines. I love you.

When Holidays Hurt
© 2014 Bo Stern

Published in Nashville, Tennessee, by Thomas Nelson. Thomas Nelson is a registered trademark of HarperCollins Christian Publishing, Inc.

Published in association with literary agent Jason Myhre of D.C. Jacobson & Associates LLC, an author management company, www.dcjacobson.com.

Italics in Scripture indicate the author's emphasis.

Unless otherwise noted, Scripture quotations are taken from HOLMAN CHRISTIAN STANDARD BIBLE. © 1999, 2000, 2002, 2003 by Broadman and Holman Publishers. All rights reserved.

Scripture quotations marked AMP are from THE AMPLIFIED BIBLE: OLD TESTAMENT. © 1962, 1964 by Zondervan (used by permission); and from THE AMPLIFIED BIBLE: NEW TESTAMENT. © 1958 by the Lockman Foundation (used by permission).

Scripture quotations marked MSG are from *The Message* by Eugene H. Peterson. © 1993, 1994, 1995, 1996, 2000. Used by permission of NavPress Publishing Group. All rights reserved.

Scripture quotations marked NIV are from Holy Bible, New International Version®, NIV®. Copyright © 1973, 1978, 1984, 2011 by Biblica, Inc™. Used by permission of Zondervan. All rights reserved worldwide. www.zondervan.com.

Scripture quotations marked NLT are from *Holy Bible*, New Living Translation. © 1996. Used by permission of Tyndale House Publishers, Inc., Wheaton, Illinois 60189. All rights reserved.

Scripture quotations marked ESV are from THE ENGLISH STANDARD VERSION. © 2001 by Crossway Bibles, a division of Good News Publishers.

Scriptures marked NASB are from NEW AMERICAN STANDARD BIBLE®. © The Lockman Foundation 1960, 1962, 1963, 1968, 1971, 1972, 1973, 1975, 1977. Used by permission.

Scriptures marked NET are from NET Bible® copyright © 1996–2006 by Biblical Studies Press, L.L.C. http://netbible.com. All rights reserved.

Scriptures marked KJV are from the King James Version of the Bible.

ISBN: 978-0-7180-1620-3

Printed in the United States of America

14 15 16 17 18 RRD 6 5 4 3 2 1

Contents

The Christmas Season

A New Year

contents

Summer and Fall

Acknowledgments

Deep thanks to the amazing crew at Thomas Nelson for being willing to take a chance on a new author's proposal for a book about the dark side of the holidays. You are brave souls and valiant visionaries, and I am honored to work with you.

To Jenn Gott for editing my words into medicine for hurting hearts and for inserting copious amounts of humor into every e-mail, knowing how much we both need to laugh. You are dearly loved.

To my agent, Jason Myhre, for the countless agency things you do that I would never, ever want to do. Ever. Thank you.

To my family, who has weathered every holiday, hard day, happy day, clinic day, in-over-our-heads day, and miraculous day with me. You make my life make sense. A million thank-yous.

To Jesus. Author and finisher, keeper and sustainer, helper and healer—all my hope is in You.

Introduction

I really loved my first forty-five Christmases. They certainly weren't perfect, but they also weren't painful. In fact, I would say that based on the purely imaginary Standard Holiday Happiness scale, although I had known highs and lows, my cumulative Christmas experience stood at a good, solid 8. I really liked holidays, and I loved making them happy for my husband and kids. It was a job I felt born to do.

Then came February 2011.

Just after celebrating our twenty-sixth wedding anniversary and on the day of our daughter's sixteenth birthday, my wonderful husband, Steve, was diagnosed with ALS (more commonly known as Lou Gehrig's disease). ALS is a disease so fierce and foul that I feared all my holidays—before and after—would be redefined by it. I imagined looking at the family picture taken when we celebrated Christmas at SeaWorld and mentally recaptioning it: *one year before our world fell apart.*

In the months after the gut punch of the initial diagnosis, I caught my breath a little. We began to get our heads around what we were facing and how we would fight it. Slowly, as spring moved into summer, we developed a new sort of normal—tentative and tender but still more secure than we had felt in the brittle winter of Steve's diagnosis.

Autumn snuck up on me with a beauty that took me by

surprise. I remember the day I gave myself permission to love it. Long drives with Steve followed as we searched for the most beautiful trees in Central Oregon and just enjoyed spending the season together with few words and much wonder. I loved fall. And I felt ready for Christmas. I really did. But as soon as the Thanksgiving leftovers were put away and the annual after-dinner Christmas movie was playing in the family room, I knew I was in trouble. Spring had been hard—appropriately hard because it was cold and the news was fresh. Summer had brought welcome warmth. Fall was lovely and peaceful. But Christmas is supposed to be *happy*. I wanted to be happy—more than anything. I wanted it for my kids and my husband and my friends, but don't let me kid you: I wanted it for *me*. I longed to fall in love with Christmas, but my broken heart had a mind of its own, and it didn't seem to understand the rules of the calendar.

Not knowing what else to do, I sat down with my Bible and outlined my options for facing my most difficult-to-date Christmas: (1) ignore it, (2) fake it, or (3) rescue it.

Option number 1 was tempting, and I probably would have chosen it if I didn't have a family depending on me for hope. Option 2 was also tempting—but impossible. I didn't have the emotional energy for it. I wasn't sure what option 3 would look like, but I wanted it. I wanted to find a way to make Christmas come alive in my broken heart and sad home. I felt desperate for Christmas to be rescued, and even though it seemed like a long shot, I decided to give it a try. I determined that instead of running from Christmas, I would instead invite Jesus into it. I would intentionally let His comfort come to my chaos by leaning *into* the swirling storm of sorrow and joy rather than away from it. And as I experienced His goodness in those tender days of Christmas, I realized I could have that goodness in all the days I would ever face as we traveled the road of suffering. In the end, the holidays of that first year post-diagnosis turned out to be some of our most beautiful.

Are you drowning in disappointment and heartache? Seasons of sorrow can easily suppress the beauty of the changing seasons and their accompanying celebrations. Holidays serve as milepost markers in our lives. We remember who we were with and what we ate and how happy everything seemed in comparison to the raw reality of right now. The problem with these built-in milestones, though, is that they're impossible to dodge. They show up every year like clockwork, woven into the rhythm of our Hallmark-card culture. We can't avoid them! But we don't have to face them alone. The real beauty of the incarnation is that Christ *came*. He came for every hard or happy day we will ever face—from weddings to winter solstice—and He promises to be near us on every single one.

Will you join me in this unlikely dance of suffering and celebration? Let's stand together for a moment—not around a perfectly Pinteresty holiday but at the foot of the cross—and look again at the Savior who was willing to step into our sorrow. There He is. For you. For us. For our sin and sadness and our breakdowns in the middle of department stores on Black Friday (oh wait, is that just me?). He *is* joy, and at the heart of His story is fullness of joy . . . *especially* for the brokenhearted.

The Christmas Season

one

Christmas in the Shadowlands

*The people who walked in darkness have seen
a great light. For those who lived in a land of
deep shadows—light! sunbursts of light!*

—Isaiah 9:2 MSG

This verse is where our story begins. Almost eight centuries before the birth of Jesus, the prophet Isaiah told of His coming. The biggest Christmas gift of all time was announced to people who would not live to see the day of its arrival. They wouldn't know the Christmas story in their lifetime. But we can know it.

Though this passage will soon tell us about Jesus, first Isaiah tells us about *us.* He paints the perfect picture of that brilliant moment when our world collides with His wonder; our darkness is pierced by His light. He didn't come to people who were already spit-shined. He came to those who were buried in darkness, desperate for help, and longing for hope.

Have you been living in the land of deep shadows? I have. I've spent long years in that gray and weary country, and sometimes it makes me feel disqualified from Christmas. Most Christmas carols do not talk about daunting shadows or dreary days. They talk sparkle and shimmer. They talk ho-ho-hoing and mistletoeing, and all of that is fine and fun if you're having a great year. But let's be honest about the fact that this relentless commercialized happiness is not really what lives at the heart of Christmas.

> *Jesus didn't come to cheer us up; He came into the shadowlands we call home to set us free.*

Christmas is deeper than that. It reaches into darker places. Jesus didn't come to cheer us up; He came into the shadowlands we call home to set us free. He came to untangle us from the despair that wraps itself around our joy and peace and purpose. It seems, then, that hopelessness is the very first qualification for receiving the bright hope of Christmas. Perhaps you are exactly where you need to be to experience the miracle of Advent after all.

Finding Hidden Hope

Today, when the sun goes down, take a candle and a match into a dark room. Sit in the darkness for a few minutes. There in the deep blue evening, consider the difficult things you are facing this Christmas. Now light the candle, and look at the way the room changes. What can you see that you couldn't see before? How does the flame flicker through the blackness that used to own the room? If you'd like, this would be a good time to start a journal where you can write down the ways you see His light invade your darkness.

. . . .

As we enter into the deep days of Advent, keep my heart focused on the real story, the only story that really matters. Send Your light to my darkness, like You did on that first Christmas, so that I can see my place in this season. With my praise and thanksgiving, I will crown You Lord of all.

two

He Came to Bring Joy

You repopulated the nation, you expanded its joy. Oh, they're so glad in Your presence! Festival joy! The joy of a great celebration, sharing rich gifts and warm greetings.

—Isaiah 9:3 MSG

Isaiah continues his version of the Christmas story here, and this verse is very exciting. Yesterday he walked us through valleys of dark shadows, but today it's like we've stumbled onto the canvas of a Norman Rockwell painting filled with joy and celebration. Think about that imagery and read the verse again. Isn't it such a beautiful picture? There was a time when I would have read a verse like this and immediately felt a weighty wave of guilt and a great deal of pressure to create this kind of scene for my family and for myself.

But read it again, because this verse is beautiful, hopeful, exciting, and . . . freeing. Let's check out the Christmas to-do list.

God's list:

- Redeem and repopulate the nation.
- Expand its joy.

My list:

- Be glad in His presence.
- Share rich gifts and warm greetings.

All the responsibility for *doing* is on Jesus. My responsibility is to experience, enjoy, and share in His beautiful gifts. Which gifts? The gift of His coming, the gift of His cross. All that we enjoy and celebrate is centered around the redemptive work of Jesus Christ—the accomplishment that provided a way for us to spend an infinite number of perfect holidays with Him in heaven. I suspect we often get so buried beneath the weight of what we're trying to create at Christmas that we miss the joy of what He *already* created.

His gift of salvation is free and it's finished. Isaiah waited and longed for it, but we *own* it. It's right in front of us . . . as real as the baby in our nativity set or the star on top of our tree. I know it's difficult to experience sorrow at Christmas, and sometimes it can feel like sorrow suffocates all hope for happiness. But this verse assures me that He can enlarge my heart so that I can also experience the joy of what He has done. Sorrow serves as a tether to His presence. It keeps us needing Him and leaning into His story. And in His story, there is joy. Finished, flowing joy.

Finding Hidden Hope

Make room in your heart today to remember His work. As you sit at a red light or wait in line at Walmart or rest your head to sleep tonight, take a minute and ten deep breaths. Breathe in the completed to-do list of Jesus. He came to save you and it *worked*. He did it. It's finished. You can rest and rejoice in that today.

. . . .

You are the God of this Christmas. I give You my list, my expectations, and my fears. I breathe in the work You started in a manger and finished on the cross. May all the cares of my whirling world find rest in You. In the name of the One who finished it all, amen.

three

He Came to Calm Confusion

His names will be: Amazing Counselor, Strong God, Eternal Father, Prince of Wholeness. His ruling authority will grow, and there'll be no limits to the wholeness he brings.

—*Isaiah 9:6 MSG*

Amazing = wonderful, miraculous.

Counselor = to advise, deliberate, or resolve.

For the next few days, we'll be opening up some gifts that are always ours because of Christmas. These gifts are not dependent on our income, intelligence, or enthusiasm. They are just as real for those who have nothing to their name as they are for those who have nothing to worry about. They are beautiful, eternal, sparkling gifts beneath the tree, and it's worth our time to lean in close and take a good look.

Isaiah tells us first about this Child who is coming to rule our world. Then he lists the Child's names, and they are stunning (and I love that Jesus is way too much for just one name). The names Isaiah ascribes to Jesus describe His character and explain why He is so qualified to rescue and redeem our lives. The first on the list is Amazing Counselor. Oh, I love this one.

The first Christmas after Steve's diagnosis with ALS, we lived in swirling uncertainty about our future. Financial decisions, life-altering medical decisions, parenting decisions, and ministry decisions swarmed around our brains like flies at a picnic. We were frustrated and failing beneath the weight of both the known and the unknown. Add to that the need to create a perfect Christmas for our family, and I thought I would drown in it all. I remember fighting tears while standing in one of the toy aisles at Target, trying to choose a set of Legos for my son and feeling paralyzed by that tiny decision. Battles are messy. Like houseguests who bring too much baggage and leave it all sitting in the entryway, it seems you can't come or go anywhere without fighting through the pile of uncertainties.

It's into this tangle of questions that He comes: our Amazing Counselor. Many translations use the word *wonderful*, which in the Hebrew means "miraculous." His arrival is a miracle. The word *counselor* means "to advise, deliberate, or resolve." Look at this comment from *Barnes' Notes*:

> The name "counselor" here, יוֹעֵץ yû'ēts, denotes one of honorable rank; one who is suited to stand near princes and kings as their adviser. It is expressive of great wisdom, and of qualifications to guide and direct the human race. The Septuagint translates this phrase, "The angel of the mighty counsel." The Chaldee, "The God of wonderful counsel."[1]

I can testify to the greatness of this gift. Into the daunting decisions of my most confusing Christmas came the Wonderful Counselor. He rode in like a knight on a white horse, and He answered so many of the questions I was facing. To those that remained unanswered, He gave the promise of His presence and the assurance that the answers would come when I needed them most.

Now, years later, I can tell you that He is still the Great Adviser I need when my wisdom is too weak for the war I face. He comes through His Word, through His presence, and through the people around me. He comes as I worship. He comes as I cry in my car because I can't find my shopping list and I don't know how I'll ever survive the toy aisle without it. He comes. He breathes life and hope, and He reminds me that not every decision is a game-changer. Oh, how thankful I am for the brilliant gift of our Amazing Counselor.

Finding Hidden Hope

Write the name *Amazing Counselor* in your journal, and beneath it list all the decisions you are facing in your battle or in your daily life. Take a moment to share your list with Him and to ask Him for miraculous help and wonderful counsel. If you feel up to it, share your list with a friend who will join you in praying for the wisdom you need.

. . . .

Great God, I confess that my wisdom is much too small for the battle I'm facing. Come in Your beauty and brilliance, come with clear direction, and I will follow. Speak Your Word that brings life and joy and safety. In the name of the only wise God, amen.

four

He Came to Rescue

*For to us a Child is born, to us a Son is given: and the
government shall be upon His shoulder, and His name
shall be called Wonderful Counselor, Mighty God,
Everlasting Father [of Eternity], Prince of Peace.*

—*Isaiah 9:6 AMP*

On the day of my husband's diagnosis, I sat in the
doctor's office and could almost *feel* the breath
of Goliath as he stood over my shoulder, shouting his
threats: "You'll never survive this. Your kids will never
survive. You've preached a blue streak about how God is
all you need, but you never imagined an enemy like this.
Your strength is no match for ALS. We might as well call
it now—you're done."

Though our giant was invisible, his presence in that
room was palpable. That night I went to bed swimming
in a mix of shock and sorrow, longing for a superhero to
ride in and rescue me. I have never felt more weak or little
or helpless than I did in that moment. I bet you've been
there too.

Battles come stocked with big giants. It's a fact. They

are large, mean, and focused on our destruction. This is why the next name of the baby born in Bethlehem is such a gift to us today:

Mighty God.

I love the word *mighty* here. It means "powerful warrior, tyrant, giant, valiant, mighty man." It seems that humble Jesus, meek and mild, has a whole lot of muscles underneath His swaddling-clothes cape. So often we overly domesticate God. We turn Him into a sweet little lap god who offers companionship and a ticket into eternity, but we forget that He is the one thing that makes our enemies tremble. Look at this:

> At every moment when I think I can't go on, I remember that I don't have to save myself.

> The LORD thundered from heaven; the Most High projected His voice. He shot His arrows and scattered them; He hurled lightning bolts and routed them. The depths of the sea became visible, the foundations of the world were exposed, at Your rebuke, LORD, at the blast of Your nostrils. He reached down from heaven and took hold of me; He pulled me out of deep waters. He rescued me from my powerful enemy and from those who hated me, for they were too strong for me. (Psalm 18:13–17)

When it comes to dealing with those who hurt His kids, He is a tyrant—a valiant, victorious, war-making God. He doesn't fit in our laps or on our mantels or in our picture frames—He is outrageously large and in charge, and we can trust Him to deal with the enemies we face.

My superhero showed up that night. And He has been showing up every night since. And every day. And every moment when I think I can't go on, can't find a way to free myself from the turmoil of battle, I remember that I don't have to save myself. We have a Savior who was built for the mission. The tiny baby came as a mighty God, and His strength is mighty to save. Merry Christmas to us!

Finding Hidden Hope

Read Psalm 66:3 out loud. What is our enemies' response to God? This verse tells us to talk to God about the ways that He is mighty. Take a minute today to speak of some of the great things He has done, and remind yourself how powerful He is for every situation you are facing during this season.

. . . .

O mighty God, I need You now. I need Your strength, Your power, and Your love to defend my broken heart and save me from the schemes of my enemies. They are too strong for me, but they are not too strong for You. Rescue me for Your name's sake I pray, amen.

five

He Came to Love

*His name shall be called Wonderful Counselor, Mighty
God, Everlasting Father [of Eternity], Prince of Peace.*

—*Isaiah 9:6 AMP*

When Steve and I began leading our first youth group, we were young and passionate, and we had a lot of ideas about transforming those kids into world-changing grown-ups nearly overnight. Our first message centered around the fact that they were children of God. Seems like a safe place to start, right? Problem: Of the fifteen kids in that group, only three had dads actually living in their home. So when we marched in all smiley and smug, saying, "God is your Father!" at least twelve of them responded with blank stares or "Who cares?"

For some of these kids, their fathers symbolized abandonment and pain. For others, their dads were just a non-entity—an empty wasteland where a real relationship should have been. We've led hundreds of teenagers since that time, and the pattern continues: we want our earthly dads to love us, but we often find they are not capable of or willing to stick it out for a long-term relationship. It's easy to transfer those feelings onto our heavenly Father, sometimes without even realizing it. No matter how you slice it, we humans long for a real relationship with a really good dad.

I love the name Everlasting Father because it tells me that when God came to us as a baby, He came to stay. He is committed to loving us in the good times, the battle times, and on into the forever times. Everlasting. From Isaiah 9 to the far reaches of eternity, He is our Father and He is good. On the most difficult days of my battle, I run for refuge to Deuteronomy 1:

> The LORD your God who goes before you will himself fight for you, just as he did for you in Egypt before your eyes, and in the wilderness, where you have seen how the LORD your God carried you, as a man carries his son, all the way that you went until you came to this place. (vv. 30–31 ESV)

As we look at the days of Advent ahead of us—the songs, the lights, the silver bells—we can trust that we are not alone. We are not orphaned or abandoned, no matter how hot our fight. He came to be our Father forever. He came to carry us when we can't face another Christmas party or open another greeting card or wrap another gift. He is our steady, strengthening Dad, holding our hands, lifting us up when our legs buckle beneath us and our hearts feel fragile and worn. He loves and cares and sees who we will be when this battle is in the history books. I'm so thankful for His everlasting, never-fading, always-perfect love.

Finding Hidden Hope

Sit by some twinkling Christmas lights with your journal, and make a list of the best qualities in a good dad. Read over the list, and know that it pales in comparison to the ways your everlasting Father loves and cares for you.

....

You are a Father to the fatherless and to the well-fathered and to everyone in between. Your love fills in the gaps dug deep by sin and sorrow and pulls us out of hiding, not to punish but to heal, not to condemn but to call. Give me faith to believe that You are good and do good—always. Amen

six

He Came for Our Peace

And he will be called Wonderful Counselor, Mighty
God, Everlasting Father, Prince of Peace.

—*Isaiah 9:6 NIV*

*P*rince of Peace.

I like the regal, royal nature of this name for the Messiah. It reminds me that this story is really about a Prince, coming to take His people back from the evil villain. This name gives me permission to be the rescued and not the rescuer. All I really have to do to qualify for redemption is to admit that I need Him. I cannot save myself from the battle I face. If I ever want to know true peace, I have to hand my life and my heartache over to the Prince of Peace. His very name marks Him as the answer to my deepest need and the hope of my days. Jesus Himself confirmed Isaiah's words:

> "Peace I leave with you; my peace I give to you. I do not give to you as the world gives. Do not let your hearts be troubled and do not be afraid." (John 14:27 NIV)

Many elements of the Christmas season feel like peace. I love the lights on my tree at night and Christmas carols and sweet baby Jesus, nestled in His bed in the nativity set. Many things, however, feel frenzied, especially if you are also in a season of battle or heartache. Noise and schedules and shoppers and pressure to buy and wrap and bake press in, and before you know it, the peace is gone from a holiday devoted to the Prince of Peace. When we take over Christmas with our own expectations and projections, we tend to move further into chaos. When *He* takes over Christmas, He brings peace. Always.

Today I'm giving myself permission to spend some time with peace. I'm going to unplug everything but the lights on my tree and listen for the sound of His footsteps as He shows up to rescue me from the chaos that battle creates. I'm giving you permission too—because not only is peace in the midst of this season possible; it's essential.

Welcome, Prince of Peace.

Finding Hidden Hope

Sit in a quiet place with your journal, and list everything about the season that brings you peace. Now list the things that make you feel tense or turbulent. Are there some items on that list that could be eliminated altogether (simplify the shopping, buy instead of bake, limit social commitments, and so on)? Close your eyes, and listen for your Prince as He comes to save you from turmoil and strife, leading you back to the heart of Christmas.

....

Jesus, I confess that I am unable to produce my own peace. In a world of churning chaos, You are my only hope, my only rest. I welcome Your government in my life and rejoice in the restoration it brings. In the name of the One who purchased my peace, amen.

seven

He Came to Multiply

*Of the increase of his government and
peace there shall be no end.*

—*Isaiah 9:7 KJV*

This sentence is the capstone to Isaiah's Christmas story. First he told us who this King would be by telling us all of His beautiful names. Now he tells us what His kingdom will look like, and it's an astounding description: constantly increasing security and peace, endless and eternal. If this is the blueprint for His kingdom, then I would like a home right in the middle of it, please.

When we find ourselves fighting on a physical, spiritual, or emotional battlefield, it's difficult to feel that our lives are increasing in security and peace. As soon as the battle lines of ALS were drawn in our family, we began to experience that claustrophobic feeling of the walls closing in as we started rationing our days and dollars and dreams so much more carefully. Everything we once held dear seemed to be slipping through our fingers. But now, as we've walked further down the road, and as we are learning to continually shift the weight of our government to His sturdy shoulders,

He is consistently proving Himself and His grand plans for our future. Look at how He does it:

> To all who mourn in Israel, he will give a crown of beauty for ashes, a joyous blessing instead of mourning, festive praise instead of despair. In their righteousness, they will be like great oaks that the LORD has planted for his own glory. (Isaiah 61:3 NLT)

Oh, this is very exciting! Isaiah has listed the raw materials God uses to provide all that we need—to bring increase to our lives. You may feel that you have nothing valuable to bring to Him. But that's okay! It turns out He needs only tears and ashes to create beauty and joy. He is so good at taking the dregs in our barrel and transforming them into something beautiful.

Your brokenness is the only material God needs in order to build something grand.

One of my biggest fears going into this battle with Steve's diagnosis was for my children, especially our eleven-year-old son. I was raised in an all-girl family, and we had three daughters before we had Josiah, so I felt desperately inadequate to be both mom and dad to that boy. How would he learn to be strong? To change a tire? To treat a lady? And what about the deeper, more important intangibles? Would he grow bitter and hard as he watched his dad suffer? Would he question the goodness of a God who would allow such suffering?

I spent hours worrying my fears up to Jesus about Josiah Stern's future. I felt like I was praying over a little pile of ashes, begging God to breathe life and hope. And He did. As the months and the story unfolded, I watched in amazement as beautiful things began to happen in the heart of that little man. A new compassion for hurting people came to life and, along with it, a passion to help raise funds to find a cure. I watched him step into brave new territory as he began to serve the dad who had once served him. He is today one of Steve's most reliable and willing helpers. And he has become a fierce fighter and advocate for the ALS community. Josiah is not being reduced by this battle. His heart is expanding, and he is rapidly increasing into the man God has always planned for him to be. It's breathtaking.

We're going to look at this treasure of a scripture again in a few days, but for today, just consider the fact that your brokenness is the only material God needs in order to build something grand. We don't have to bring Him perfect plans, perfect prayers, or perfect peace—we just bring our own sad selves, and He does all the work.

Can you trust Him with your brokenness today? Can you believe that out of the pain of your battle could come endless security and peace? Believe it, friend. It's for you He came.

Finding Hidden Hope

Close your eyes and hold out your hands in front of you as you think of all the things in your life that feel insecure or depleted this Christmas. Now extend your hands to Him, and ask Him to use these very things as the ingredients for increase. You'll be amazed at what He can do with a government that is given over to His goodness.

....

God of all I need, I bring You my heartache, knowing that only You can breathe something beautiful into the mess. In my attempts to analyze the fire that caused the ashes, I confess that I have undervalued Your ability to re-create them. But Your promise of new, increased life is unconditional and unending, so it's to You I come. In the name of the One who makes all things new, amen.

eight

He Came to Bring Good News

*The Spirit of the Lord God is upon me, because the Lord
has anointed and qualified me to preach the Gospel of
good tidings to the meek, the poor, and afflicted.*

—Isaiah 61:1 AMP

I love a good Christmas movie as much as the next girl, but I secretly suspect they're responsible for many of our misconceptions about the meaning of Christmas. In addition to the obvious twisting of the story from Jesus to Santa and angels to elves, movies often portray an interesting view of our relationship with God. Generally, when a family goes to church for a Christmas Eve service in the movies, they are dressed to the nines. They wear suits and dresses, and they warn their fresh-faced kids to be on their best behavior because "this is *God's* house!"

While I think a certain amount of decorum in a worship service is appropriate, I don't see much polish in the actual Christmas story. Read the verse at the top again. Isaiah 61 is one of the most well-known prophecies about our Messiah's arrival. First it tells us why He will come, and then this beautiful proclamation tells us *to whom* He will come. And who are these people who will be the recipients of the best news in all of history? The successful and spiffed up? Nope. The wealthy and winning? Also no. Isaiah tells us that Jesus' target audience is the meek, the poor, and the afflicted. Quite an illustrious group, yes? Most of us would not choose to include those labels on our résumés, but they're the very words Isaiah chooses to describe those who are the object of Jesus' affection. Essentially he tells us that even though everyone needs to be rescued, our Savior is coming for those who *know* they need to be rescued.

Isaiah warns us that this is Jesus' mission, and then Jesus confirms it Himself in Mark 2:17: "When Jesus heard this, he told them, 'Healthy people don't need a doctor—sick people do. I have come to call not those who think they are righteous, but those who know they are sinners'" (NLT). Just as we saw on day one, our Hero came to rescue those sitting in darkness—the sorry lots who knew they were dead without Him. He came for those of us in trouble, in sorrow, in poverty, and in pain. The Christmas story is all about His beauty coming full-tilt into our battlefield.

Maybe this is the year to see through the polished-up holiday veneer and remember the promise of Isaiah. Christ has come . . . to our crisis, our calamity, and our Christmas. He comes with good news of great joy that will bring gifts of hope and gladness as we unwrap them. He is here for you. Receive Him.

Finding Hidden Hope

Take a quiet minute, and listen to the old Christmas carol "O Come, O Come, Emmanuel." When we hear these classic songs, we typically tend to focus on Jesus coming to redeem all humanity. This time, however, focus your heart entirely on the fact that He came for you, right where you are, right in this moment. Let this knowledge disperse the clouds and put death's dark shadows to flight!

. . . .

You came for the poor and wounded and wanting. You came for me. Help me to see my place in Your story and in Your heart. Help me to understand the full measure of Your grace. In the name of the One who came to seek and save, amen.

nine

He Came to Our Broken Dreams

Now the birth of Jesus Christ took place under these circumstances:
When His mother Mary had been promised in marriage to
Joseph, before they came together, she was found to be pregnant
[through the power] of the Holy Spirit. And her (promised)
husband Joseph, being a just and upright man and not willing
to expose her publicly and to shame and disgrace her, decided
to repudiate and dismiss (divorce) her quietly and secretly.

—*Matthew 1:18–19 AMP*

Today our story takes us to Israel, sometime around AD 2 or 3. Eight hundred years after Isaiah prophesied that a child would come and take over the frail and failing government, the Jewish people were still waiting, watching, and praying for rescue. They were hoping for a hero from royal bloodlines who would ride in on a white horse and save them from the Roman Empire. They were *not* looking for an illegitimate baby from a rough-and-tumble neighborhood. Though other cultures had claimed that their heroes had been born of virgins, it was unprecedented and unanticipated in Hebrew culture.[2]

The Christmas story really is charming only in hindsight. From our vantage point, all the pieces fit perfectly in history just like the figures fit snugly in our nativity sets. But read the first line in today's verse again because it is a weighty sentence: "Now the birth of Jesus occurred *under these circumstances.*" Under what circumstances? A fresh look at the people involved reminds us that this situation is as real and raw as they come. In fact, the most amazing event our world has ever known began as a big, ugly scandal.

Innocent Mary is suddenly pregnant, and there is no reason for anyone (including her beloved) to believe it's the result of anything other than her own unfaithfulness and sin. Joseph, a good and kind man, doesn't deserve this betrayal and embarrassment. So even before the story gets off the ground, our heroes are dealing with ruined reputations, destroyed credibility, and broken trust. In addition, Mary is peering into her future as an unwed mother in a society that is not kind to any women, much less those of ill repute. Despite what she knows to be true about God's purpose in this process, I would imagine that her head and heart were spinning pretty fast.

So these are the circumstances—the first pages of the story of Jesus. As we'll see in the days to come, there's not

> Jesus, the only human in history with the power to write His own birth story, chose a broken one. He chose to enter our timeline low—maybe so we all could reach Him.

a single perfect thing about it. Isaiah predicted that Jesus would be a man who was "despised and rejected—a man of sorrows, acquainted with deepest grief" (Isaiah 53:3 NLT). Have you ever wondered why? Jesus could have just as easily rescued our world had He come from a wealthy two-parent home with stellar social standing. And yet Jesus, the only human in history with the power to write His own birth story, chose a broken one. He chose to enter our timeline low—maybe so we all could reach Him.

As I look at the characters of Advent, I think of my own story, and I feel right at home. Like Mary, my future is also uncertain and my family doesn't feel as perfectly pristine as those on the Target commercials. And yet here in the middle of this sorrow, we are making room for the arrival of the Son of God. We know He will fit right in because He is not afraid of our grief. He is acquainted with it. If He didn't avoid it in His own story, I can be certain He won't avoid it in ours.

Let's make a pact today that, when we look around at the bells and whistles of Christmas and when we feel alienated from all that happy, we'll remember that we fit just fine in the first story. The *real* story. There, in that story, our sorrow finds a home among friends, and our brokenness finds a Savior who understands. It's a beautiful place to begin and a lovely place to live.

Finding Hidden Hope

Take a walk today, and breathe in a fresh perspective on the birth story of Jesus. How can you relate to His life and family?

. . . .

Dear Jesus, thank You for choosing to come into our world and to come in low so all of us could reach You. Thank You for setting aside Your right to rule with an iron fist and for instead winning the world with love. You are my joy today. Amen

ten

He Speaks into Sorrow

But after he had considered these things, an angel of the
Lord suddenly appeared to him in a dream, saying, "Joseph,
son of David, don't be afraid to take Mary as your wife,
because what has been conceived in her is by the Holy
Spirit. She will give birth to a son and you are to name Him
Jesus, because He will save His people from their sins."

— *Matthew 1:20–21*

Every time I read this part of the story, my heart aches for Joseph. I wonder what his dreams looked like before his life took such a hairpin turn. Had he dreamt of the love he would share with Mary or about the night he would make her his own? Had he imagined their children, their home, or the secrets they would whisper in the dark? Joseph was a real man with real dreams, and I would imagine that at this moment in his life, those long-held desires lay in ruins around his feet. Nothing was going the way he had imagined it would go. Can you relate?

It's beautiful to me that God doesn't speak to awake, alert, and conscious Joseph; He speaks into his dreams. He sends angelic comfort to his broken heart, and we can get a clue as to Joseph's emotional condition from the very first words the angel speaks: "Don't be afraid to take Mary as your wife, because what has been conceived in her is by the Holy Spirit." God steps into Joseph's story to tell him that the problem they are facing contains divine possibilities. The problem is painful, yes, and there's no denying it, but it is also filled with purpose.

Perhaps you're way ahead of me and you know that I'm going to suggest that the Holy Spirit might also want to speak into *your* broken dreams and broken heart this Christmas. And maybe you've already decided why that's impossible. You've looked at the landscape of your sorrow and sifted through the soil of your battlefield, and you are certain there is no possible redemptive purpose lurking there. But . . . what if?

> He is more beautiful to me than He has ever been because I need Him more than I ever have.

What if God has a word to speak into your pain that might give light and courage to the way you face it? I'm not suggesting that His purpose will invalidate your pain, because so many of the things we suffer in this fallen world are not the perfect will of God—our enemy is rotten and relentless in his determination to steal, kill, and destroy. So it's not that we are asking God to remove the sting of sorrow, but rather to help us see how He can use it to produce eternal beauty in us.

The beauty that has come from my sorrow (so far) includes a whole new level of compassion, a deeper and more unshakable trust in God's character, a fresh credibility with a dying world, and a fiercely intentional strategy for living life with no regrets. Would I trade these things for my husband's health? Honestly, no, I don't think I would. I still feel that ALS is not God's perfect will for Steve or for anyone. But I will rejoice in the comfort I have experienced through the turmoil and in the way our Father is being glorified because of it. Bottom line: I know Him better now than I did before. He is *my* God. He is *my* Friend. He is more beautiful to me than He has ever been because I need Him more than I ever have.

Today, as we head deeper into the heart of Christmas, consider the ways God is speaking into your broken dreams. Ask Him for truth that will silence lies and for comfort that will surround your sorrow. Let's join with Joseph, facing the battle with courage and strength, knowing that He makes beautiful things out of messy material.

Finding Hidden Hope

Read Revelation 21:3–5 out loud. One of the reasons Jesus came to dwell with us—and is coming again—is to wipe away every tear. Every single tear. Have you put off crying this season? Trying to hold in the tears and keep it together? Maybe now is a good time to let them flow and let Him meet you in your sorrow and dwell with you there for a bit.

. . . .

God of my deepest, dearest dreams, thank You for letting me be honest with You. It is astounding that our tears are treasured by You, stored up in Your bottle, perhaps for that glorious day in eternity when we'll have to be reminded that we ever cried at all. In the name of Your Son, who understands our sorrow, amen.

eleven

He Came to Be Close to Us

*Now all this took place to fulfill what was spoken by
the Lord through the prophet: See the virgin will become
pregnant and give birth to a son, and they will name Him
Immanuel, which is translated "God is with us."*

—*Matthew 1:22–23*

I am not a good housekeeper. In fact, when my kids were little, the sight of the vacuum emerging from a tangled coat closet was always met with confused stares and the immediate question: "Who's coming over?"

Though not everyone hates housework like I do, I think most of us could confess to an area in our lives where we feel the need to keep our best foot forward. Maybe it's our work life or love life or friend life or family life. No matter what it is, there's usually something hunkered down in a dark corner of our heart whispering, "If people knew this about me, they would disappear."

When our battle started, I feared that my friends who were so wonderfully supportive initially would get tired of it over the long haul. A terminal disease is ugly to look at, and I (wrongly) worried they would move on to happier, healthier friends, and then I felt pressured to pretend that things were better than they were. It's often the fear of being alone that keeps us showing our cleaned-up, covered-over selves to the world. It's a lot of work. And the irony is that having friends who love the fake you isn't much less lonely than having no friends at all.

Herein lies the deep, dense beauty of today's passage, *Immanuel*. His very name speaks of His character. His name speaks of His location. What is His location? With us. With who? With *you*. Wherever you are, in whatever condition, cleaned up or burned out, He comes right into the heart of your fight.

Psalm 34 tells us that God is near "to the brokenhearted and saves those who are crushed in spirit" (v. 18 NIV). Jesus is not afraid of our pain or sorrow. He doesn't run from a needy friend. Jesus was built for battle, and He shows up on time, every time, bringing comfort with Him (Matthew 5:4).

The world was a mess on the first Christmas night, but Jesus came. He came wearing a name of endless hope and promise: *with us*. God is with us when the money runs out, with us when the bad news comes, with us when the holiday isn't happy, and with us when everyone else disappears. The question this Christmas is not, "Will Jesus show up?" The question is, "Will I receive Him, even if He's all I have?"

Today is a good day to give yourself permission to be the real you in front of the real God. You don't have to hide your hurt or sin away. He comes to heal, to save, and to rescue. Let earth receive her king.

Finding Hidden Hope

Is loneliness nipping at your heart today? Write *Immanuel* on your hand or on a sticky note you will see often to remind yourself that He is the God who shows up.

....

Dear Immanuel, You are the God who comes. To all my beauty and all my battle, You show up and You are enough. I choose to believe it and to make a place for You, right here with me. In the name of the One who is with us, amen.

twelve

He Blesses Obedience

*When Joseph got up from sleeping, he did as the Lord's angel
had commanded him. He married her, but did not know her
intimately until she gave birth to a son. And he named Him Jesus.*

—*Matthew 1:24–25*

These small verses contain two distinctly important
points of obedience on Joseph's part and give us great
insight into his character. First he married the girl he had
just decided to divorce. Joseph hitched his cart to the enor-
mous and life-changing call of God on Mary's life. He said
yes to becoming the stepdad to a King. This was big, brave
obedience.

Perhaps not as brave but still significant is that Joseph
followed through and named the baby Jesus. Joseph doesn't
usually get a lot of credit in the Christmas story, but at the
heart of it all, he heard God clearly and obeyed Him completely—even though life was not turning out exactly as he
had expected. That's big.

Obedience can be tricky to pull off in the best circumstances, but when a fierce battle is raging, it can seem
impossible. Unfair even. Why would God ask me to do

something more when I'm already overwhelmed with the hand I've been dealt? And here's another tough truth about hard seasons: they're *noisy*. Emotions rage, sorrow screams, and clamoring thoughts collide against each other, creating a relentless inner cacophony that can make it seem impossible to hear the still, small voice of Immanuel.

> *Sometimes we need to close out the noise of the season in order to spend a little time with the Source of the season.*

And yet . . . in spite of all these things, I've found the best strategy for facing any battle is: pray, listen, obey. It's become a mantra of mine when I feel the world is caving in and I'm not sure what to do next. I speak it out loud into my situation: *pray, listen, obey.* I find a quiet spot, even if that means going to my car for a minute and shutting myself in with no friends and no noise, just

Jesus. Sometimes we need to close out the noise of the season in order to spend a little time with the Source of the season. I've discovered that most often, when I think God has gone missing from my situation, it's actually that I've been too stressed to see or hear Him. A moment of quiet is usually all it takes to be reminded that He is there, waiting to be welcomed in.

This is a good time to ask: Are there any areas of delayed obedience in your life that might be making your battle more difficult? If there's anything you know you need to do before you can move forward, why not take the step today? Now. It's always the right time to get unstuck. The God who loves you would also love to lead you, and you can trust that His instructions are always worth obeying. His love will guide you safely through this season and into all that will follow.

Having trouble hearing God's voice today? I'm wishing for you a quiet place and a quiet heart. Beyond wishing, I'm praying for it and believing that the One who loves you so much will flood your heart with His presence and will water the dry, weary ground with words of life.

> It's always the right time to get unstuck.

Finding Hidden Hope

Just for today, commit to a quiet car and, if possible, a quiet house. Spend some time in the solitude with your journal, and write down anything you hear God speaking as you focus on His presence and His voice.

. . . .

In this season filled with clamorous noise and crowded calendars, I want to make time and room to hear Your voice. Your words are life to me. Your direction is all I need. Give me ears to hear and a heart to obey. In the name of the One who brings quiet rest, amen.

thirteen

He Multiplies Our Yes

*And Mary said: My soul proclaims the greatness of the Lord,
and my spirit has rejoiced in God my Savior, because He has
looked with favor on the humble condition of His slave. Surely,
from now on all generations will call me blessed, because the
Mighty One has done great things for me, and His name is holy.*

—*Luke 1.46–49*

I've read this story so many times, but I'm always
amazed as young Mary steps onto history's stage with
such grace and dignity. It's impossible to understand the mag-
nitude of her yes here, especially in this very moment, when
she could see generations down the road, having the angel's
assurance that she would be called *blessed*, but couldn't see
days down the road to know whether Joseph would choose
to stay or to go. Her current reputation and all her future
dreams are suddenly lashed to the altar of sacrifice, and she
has no way of knowing whether they will live or die.

When Mary accepts the angel's proposal, she isn't just
submitting to the will of God; she is submitting to it at the
exclusion of all other options and expectations. And her
decision tips over a long row of dominoes waiting in the

wings behind it. For Mary, the angel's visit made the hallowed moment in the stable possible, but it also triggered the harrowing moment at the cross. This kind of obedience and blind trust is stunning, and it is required of all of us, not just those called to carry the Messiah.

It used to be that when I would dream about my future, it was mostly about the things God would add to my life. I didn't often imagine the takeaways, but I'm old enough now to realize that usually there are both. When I said yes to Steve Stern in 1985, the bullet points were very clear: in sickness and health, in poverty and wealth, to love and to cherish till death do us part. These were the things I could see. I couldn't see the children and grandchildren that were wrapped up in our yeses that day. I couldn't see the hundreds of teenagers we would love and pastor together. I couldn't see the jobs we would lose or the mistakes we would make. I couldn't see the day I would become Steve's caregiver in addition to being his wife. That one yes led to so much joy and sorrow, and I don't think our story is unique.

> *The will of God often involves beautiful and brutal. Good and hard. Happy and sad.*

The will of God often involves beautiful and brutal. Good and hard. Happy and sad. It would all feel like a dizzying dance if not for Mary's final line:

The Mighty One has done great things for me, and His name is holy.

Unless we can fully trust His greatness, we'll always be tempted to fall back on our own good ideas or our own muscle in seasons of battle. The holiness of His name and the sovereignty of His will trumps all other winning and losing. It levels every playing field, fills in every dip in the road, and heals every heart. He doesn't do good things, only great things. So we can rest in the knowledge that His love will prevail and the long nights will bow to fresh mornings.

Holy is His name.

Perfect are His plans.

In this we will rejoice.

Finding Hidden Hope

What is the most important yes you have ever said? What was the result? Is there a yes to be said today? Take a moment alone today, and ask our good God to show you how His sovereignty has covered and carried you through this season of battle.

. . . .

Sovereign God, despite the racing and rushing of this season, I say yes to Your coming. Give me the strength and wisdom to clear away the clutter to make room for Your will and all it contains. Grant that my small yes would enable new life to flow into my wounded world. In the name of the One who said yes to me, amen.

fourteen

He Satisfies

Jesus answered, "Everyone who drinks this water will be thirsty again, but whoever drinks the water I give them will never thirst. Indeed, the water I give them will become in them a spring of water welling up to eternal life."

—John 4:13–14 NIV

Christmas 2012 was perfect, really, as perfect as a holiday could be considering the very obvious battle my family was fighting. The gifts were just right. The food was delicious (thank you, Food Network). Our home was warm and sparkly.

Perfect.

And yet something was missing. As I got in bed Christmas Eve and pulled the covers around my chin, I felt it seeping in: an aching void, an agitated discontent, an unnamed, unwanted Christmas intruder. *Melancholy.*

Tossing and turning, I tried to throw the bum out, tried to reason it out, tried to focus-on-the-great-night it out. But still melancholy churned a river inside me. Was it regret that the holiday was nearly over? Frustration at the not-quite-right things? Envy of other families enjoying Christmas Eve free of a terminal illness and all the uncertainty it brings? I asked myself these honest, painful questions, hoping to quickly get beyond the feelings of gray, murky midnight that grew more suffocating by the minute. But the more I thought, the more frustrated I became.

Then it came, something I had been studying for the past few weeks. It wafted in like the song down in Whoville, and it hit my heart hard at first (maybe hard enough to crack the resilient shell I had constructed to deal with all the emotions of the holiday), and then in soft waves of bubbling solace, it came full force into my weary spirit:

"If anyone is thirsty, let him come to Me and drink." (John 7:37 NASB)

Over and over it rolled. *Are you thirsty? Come to Me.* No conditions or prequalifications. No caveats or consolations. Just Jesus. The only true satisfaction. The only lasting life.

Why doesn't a perfectly perfect Christmas satisfy? I honestly have no idea. It looks really good on paper. All I know for sure is that this churning thirst has stirred in me in varying degrees for all the holidays I can remember, not just the difficult ones. Each has held a thrilling high followed by a drop of some degree. Sometimes the drop is small and sometimes it's huge, but it's always been there, just on the other side of what I thought had been perfect. The only explanation I can come up with is this: Christmas might sometimes thrill us, but it can never really fill us.

"Come to Me and drink."

This beautiful line was not spoken by Jesus; it was *shouted* by Jesus. In fact, the Greek word is *ekraxen*—"to scream or cry out." Jesus stood in the middle of the masses that had gathered "on the greatest day of the feast" (sounds like our Christmas, yes?), and He yelled at the top of His lungs to the people He loved, "Here I am! I'm here to fill you! Come to Me for a long, tall drink of satisfaction."

This same idea was prophesied by Isaiah, long before Jesus came in the flesh:

> "Come, all you who are thirsty, come to the waters; and you who have no money, come, buy and eat! Come, buy wine and milk without money and without cost." (Isaiah 55:1 NIV)

Do you hear the passion in those words? The prophet is nearly begging us to take advantage of this beautiful gift. He knows we are weary travelers in a parched land, wandering through the wilderness of our world, hoping to stumble on the one thing that will give us rest and refreshment. Isaiah offers us the solution by asking us to come, to move toward the source of life. Eight centuries later, Jesus repeats the offer to the people in Jerusalem.

And two thousand years after that, on a sad Christmas Eve, He extended the invitation to me as well. It sounded like a whisper, but He must have been shouting to be heard through the tumult of my noisy thoughts. From somewhere outside my tiny, temporary bubble of reality, He yelled a lifeline to me. "You're not sad, Bo. You're just thirsty. Come to Me."

I'm so thankful for access to the one and only well that never, never, never runs dry. And I'm thankful for a Christmas Eve that leads me there. Has a nearly perfect or less-than-perfect or not-at-all-perfect holiday season left you wanting more? Go to Him. He's good at filling empty hearts with fresh hope that lasts.

Finding Hidden Hope

Grab a journal or a piece of blank paper, and write a list of everything you have hope for—even if you mostly just hope to make it through this day. Write it down and then hold it up to God as you ask for His hope to meet you in this new season.

. . . .

You are the God of life and death, of empty and full. You leave nothing undone and no one unloved. You see; You hear; You heal. Because these things are true of You, You are our hope. You only. You completely. You presently, and You eternally. And we are satisfied. Amen.

A New Year

fifteen

Dreaming Hard on the Longest Nights

Yet this I call to mind and therefore I have hope: Because of the LORD's great love we are not consumed, for his compassions never fail. They are new every morning; great is your faithfulness. I say to myself, "The LORD is my portion; therefore I will wait for him."

—*Lamentations 3:21–24 NIV*

My grandfather died when my grandmother was in her early sixties. I remember my mom saying, "She's so young to be a widow." I also remember how the sorrow quickly, permanently etched its way into weary lines on Grandma's face. She did not enjoy life without my granddad.

I stayed with her one weekend during winter solstice. As we cooked pancakes together in her tiny kitchen, she sighed long and heavy and said, "Winter solstice is the saddest day of the year." I had never heard anyone express opinions of any sort about winter solstice, so I asked her why she felt that way. She shook her head in exasperation, thinking everyone should know the answer to the question. When she spoke, her tone was filled with sadness rimmed with a hint of bitter:

"Because it's the shortest day and the longest night of the year. I hate nights." Such an emphatic, inclusive declaration: *I hate nights*. All nights. It seemed so extreme. I was young and in college. My days were for working, and my nights were for playing. In fact, nighttime was definitely the best part of my day. I couldn't imagine why anyone would not like nights.

I understand my grandmother so much better now. During seasons of battle, nights can be long and lonely. They can feel shaky and tenuous and sometimes even dangerous. For those of us locked in a soul-shaking struggle, our need to constantly keep moving, keep working to end the war, is intense. Nighttime puts a halt to our ability to manage and manipulate and moves life into an agonizing, slow-motion crawl. Our action is suspended. Our doing is done. All we can do is wait while all the happy people sleep. And wait. Psalm 130 is a song of ascents—one of the songs sung as the children of Israel made their way up to Jerusalem. In it, they sing out my heart with this haunting line:

> I wait for the LORD more than watchmen wait for the morn-
> ing, more than watchmen wait for the morning. (v. 6 NIV)

Why do they sing that line twice? I think because they mean it twice. Once just isn't enough to express the depths of their longing as they wait for the Lord. The watchman waits for the end of danger and the end of darkness. When morning comes, he's free to go back to his wife and his home and his happy life. He's free to finally rest. No wonder he waits with such eager anticipation.

Enduring a long battle can feel like waiting for that moment when the sun finally pierces through the inky sky and we are able to set down our weapons and welcome the day. Because I haven't found any secrets for speeding up the sunrise, I've had to look for ways to invite the comfort of God into the very long, very dark nights. These words from the prophet Micah have become a night-light:

Though I have fallen, I will rise. Though I sit in darkness, the LORD will be my light. (Micah 7:8 NIV)

And this, from King David:

When I think of You as I lie on my bed, I meditate on You during the night watches because You are my helper; I will rejoice in the shadow of Your wings. (Psalm 63:6–7)

As I whisper these verses over and over, the darkness begins to take on the shape of His shadow. It no longer swallows me up in the black abyss but rather surrounds me like a warm blanket on a cold night. In the darkness there is solitude. In the darkness there is intimacy. In the darkness there is quiet. And it's there God can speak.

If you find yourself today in a seemingly endless winter solstice, take heart. Morning will come. Joy will break through the darkness. The sunrise can't be stopped any more than gravity can be suspended. But until it comes, there is beauty to be found in the longest nights and the hardest fights. Believe it.

Finding Hidden Hope

Write out the verses from this chapter, and put them beside your bed for when the night gets long. Better yet, memorize them, letting them take up permanent residence in your heart and head so comfort is always at the ready while you wait for the sunrise.

....

God of night and day, You are light in my darkness and peace in my restlessness. Your shadow surrounds me with grace. With truth. With all that I need to wait with hope. You will send morning because You are true to Your Word. But until then, I will learn to dance in the dark, knowing that You are watching and loving and keeping me safe. Amen.

sixteen

Daring to Imagine a Brand-New Year

Delayed hope makes the heart sick, but
fulfilled desire is a tree of life.

—Proverbs 13:12

Call me a party scrooge, but I think there are a lot of things to hate about New Year's Eve—starting with the fact that it's a couples holiday and ending with "Auld Lang Syne," which seems like a sad song for a happy occasion. Even when we were young and Steve was healthy, I found myself feeling despondent on New Year's Eve, and I've only recently pinned down the reason why: the countdown.

We work our way to midnight, an hour I never actually witness on any other day. We wait and eat too much and look toward that one magical moment when the clock strikes midnight and 5 . . . 4 . . . 3 . . . 2 . . . 1 . . .

It's a minute later than it was before. Fireworks crackle, confetti flies, kisses all around, but I am not fooled inside: my life is the same life it was before the bells rang. The countdown is a letdown.

I've crafted a fair amount of countdowns of my own,

though I don't ever label them as such. They usually begin with the words "As soon as I . . ." As soon as I get married, life will be good. As soon as we buy a house, I'll feel like a success. As soon as I have a child . . . get a promotion . . . take that dream vacation . . . fix my marriage. The countdowns can wear a lot of faces, but each will eventually resolve in one of three stories:

1. The dream came true, and it's every bit as incredible as I thought it would be.
2. The dream came true, and it's nothing like I thought it would be.
3. The clock just kept ticking into oblivion.

Scenarios two and three are infinitely more common in our real lives than the first. Putting a timer on an achievement or life change is not like timing the Thanksgiving turkey. It's not an exact science, and it sets us up for disappointment and discouragement over and over.

Buried in the pages of the psalms are many keys to living a fulfilled, satisfied life, but Psalm 37 is my very favorite. I know that this verse is written on many greeting cards and cross-stitched on many pillows, but if we choose to read it through the lens of our deferred hopes and dreams, it becomes a fresh and powerful weapon in the battle with unmet expectations:

Trust in the LORD and do what is good; dwell in the land and live securely. Take delight in the LORD, and He will

give you your heart's desires. . . . Be silent before the
LORD and wait expectantly for Him. (vv. 3–4, 7)

Something powerful happens when we shift the weight
of our expectations away from the fulfillment of our own
dreams and set it fully on the God of all dreams. The older
I get, the more I am experiencing the fulfillment of some
expectations I never realized I had. He keeps proving to me
that He knows better than I what will bring satisfaction and
what will truly enable me to build a home in a secure land.
As we set our hope in His character, we can trust that He is
in control of all the countdown clocks.

If I'm being honest, the second part of the verse is much
harder for me. I'm not good at silent, and I'm not good at waiting. Often I find that even when my mouth is quiet, my mind
is talking a blue streak about what I want, what I need, why
I deserve it, and when I would like it to show up. That's why
I think this instruction is so important. Learning to focus
exclusively on who God is—without telling Him what we
think He should be doing with His omnipotence—is a valuable skill. Meditating on His unending faithfulness and love
fills us with faith for the future and creates a safe haven of
rest in our spirit. My mind is often set on fast-forward, planning the next move, the next meal, the next hill to take. Like
a constantly ticking stopwatch, my expectations are noisy
and can easily rob me of the ability to experience the sacred
space of solitude. As I discipline myself to let His voice be the
only one in the room, my anxious thoughts are quieted, and
my heart fills with the kind of hope that does not disappoint.

If facing another New Year's Eve countdown is filling you with dread, take some time to focus your attention on the One who lives outside of time, space, and Times Square. His plans for the year ahead are safe, and His dreams will not disappoint. You can count on it.

Finding Hidden Hope

Give yourself the gift of time today: twenty uninterrupted minutes. Now add to that time the gift of silence, and add to the silence thoughts focused exclusively on God's goodness. Thank Him for life and breath. Thank Him for running water. Listen for His voice, and then write down what you hear. It might just become your road map for the year ahead.

. . . .

God of this year, my heart is a cacophony of dreams, fears, and questions. I'm dizzy with trying to figure it out, to figure You out. As I seek You in silence, please meet me with Your grace. Cover me with Your kindness. You are my hope, my life, my all. Amen.

seventeen

Dreaming on the Battlefield

In their hearts, humans plan their course,
but the LORD establishes their steps.

—Proverbs 16:9 NIV

I have a dream. It's a dream that ALS will one day be eradicated in this world. I have a dream that no man will ever have to spend a beautiful summer day in a wheelchair, muscles caving in around him, while his friends go golfing. I have a dream that no boy will ever have to feed his dad breakfast because his arms are too weak to lift a spoon. This dream is so big and so real that sometimes I think it has me. I am undone over the injustice that is amyotrophic lateral sclerosis. It makes me sad. It makes me mad. It makes me get moving. Diseases need scientists and doctors, but they also need storytellers. And telling the world the story of the victims of ALS is my passion.

The thing is, while I consider this one of the defining dreams of my life, I've had it for only a few years. The diagnosis has been a problem much longer. The first recorded case of ALS was in 1869. America has known about ALS at least since the days of Lou Gehrig, who died seventy-five years ago. I'd like to say I grew to care about this cause because my heart is so big and compassionate for all people who suffer with this disease, but that wouldn't be true. This dream was born the minute I realized the man I love the most would suffer from it. It was born on our battlefield.

I wonder: What would Martin Luther King Jr.'s dream have been had he been born an upper-class white kid from Vermont? Would he perhaps have been another wealthy and well-educated politician, fighting for lower taxes and better roads? There's something about experiencing a great injustice that gives us a unique passion and credibility to fight it. In his most famous speech—a speech that has shaped our culture and our future—King refers to his people, "sadly crippled by the manacles of segregation and the chains of discrimination." He talks about those living on a "lonely island of poverty in the midst of a vast ocean of material prosperity." These emotional word pictures were not crafted from a position of comfort and privilege; they were developed in the salt mines of personal suffering and pain. They were rooted in the soil of Martin Luther King Jr.'s own battlefield.

> *Though battle nearly always alters the course of our dreams, I believe it can be the birthplace for a brand-new dream.*

When I was growing up, I wanted to be the first female NFL quarterback. When that dream (thankfully) died, I

64

wanted to be a scientist. When I discovered I hated math, I wanted to be a lawyer. I never dreamed I would become a storyteller for the victims of a disease, but now that I'm here, I wouldn't have it any other way. God has used the force of our fight to shape my dream into His dream. He has developed gifts in my life along the way that will help drive the dream. And by watching my dear husband live at the mercy of such a vicious villain, I have developed the necessary passion to give my time and energy to this fight. God is using our battle to build us into those who have the credibility to fight well for others who suffer.

Though battle nearly always alters the course of our dreams, I believe it can be the birthplace for a brand-new dream. Proverbs reiterates this:

Many are the plans in a person's heart, but it is the LORD's purpose that prevails. (19:21 NIV)

I had plotted and planned my course for forty-five years when the Lord suddenly and significantly altered it. He steered my heart and my dreams in the direction of His heart. I never would have chosen it, but I wouldn't trade it for anything. And though a cure for ALS looks impossible right now, MLK Day gives me hope that anything can happen when we give our plans and hands to God to use.

As we take this day to remember and celebrate Martin Luther King Jr.'s beautiful, impossible, finally-coming-true dream, take some time to review the course of your battle. Has it inspired a new dream? Revived an old one? Is there a cause you care about that you didn't before? Rather than dreaming only of getting off the battlefield, dare to expand your thinking and ask our great God how He might use your passion, compassion, and credibility to serve a purpose bigger than you've ever dreamed. You'll never regret it.

Finding Hidden Hope

Read a transcript of Martin Luther King Jr.'s "I Have a Dream" speech (it's easy to find online). If you're feeling inspired and creative, grab a journal and write a speech of your own.

. . . .

O great Refiner and Reviver of dreams, I give You all of mine. May my time on this battlefield become a beauty to behold and a glory to Your name. Give me eyes to see what only You can and a heart to feel Your compassion for a world I may have overlooked in the past. Direct my steps, alter my course, invade my dreams. In the name of the One who makes everything possible, amen.

eighteen

Dreaming in the Hallmark Aisle

I am my beloved's and my beloved is mine.

—Song of Solomon 6:3 NIV

I have an amazing support group of ALS wives from all over the country. We "meet" each day through e-mail, sharing experiences, ideas, encouragement, hope, and sorrow. We pray for each other constantly, but especially when a husband is approaching the final stretch of road between here and heaven. So far, we've wept and rejoiced for the three wives in our group who have safely placed their men into the arms of Jesus. Barring something supernatural, each of us knows that we will soon be living the same story.

I recently asked these wives about the difficult situations they had encountered as they walked through the battle of ALS. Several of them mentioned an event that I agree has been extremely painful, but I wouldn't have thought of it on my own: shopping for a card for Valentine's Day.

So much changes in the nature of a marriage during the course of a terminal illness. Some things are better, many things are worse, but we all agree: it's not the same. The card I would have chosen for my husband when he was healthy and our future was bright does not seem appropriate now. In fact, it's remarkable how many cards cut into my emotions like a knife.

I used to love Valentine's Day, but now it just sort of annoys me. It reminds me of a time when love was fresh and young and anything was possible. It takes me back to crazy weekend getaways and passionate fights and hard-won victories. My memories are still meaningful, but they've been reshaped as I view them through the lens of a future I couldn't see coming then. Consequently, instead of feeling young and in love during romantic holidays, I feel old and exhausted. I think Steve feels the same way (but he's really good about making sure flowers show up at my office on special days).

For so many reasons, holidays that center around romance can be painful reminders of love lost or love not-yet-found. Those who are still waiting for "the one" to ride in on a white horse and sweep them off their feet do not enjoy the moment the ball drops on New Year's Eve as they look around awkwardly for someone to high-five at midnight. All holidays tend to mark our journey. They are mileposts that show us how much ground has been gained or lost in the past year. But the romantic, relationshippy holidays just naturally group people into Has Love and Has Not Love categories.

> I'm convinced that our emptiest days can create a conduit for our fullest full.

Although I don't have any tricks for feeling happy on a lonely or difficult Valentine's Day, I do have a go-to verse for just such occasions. This verse is an anchor for my soul and hope for all the holidays I will face in the future. It's simple and to the point:

> I am my beloved's, and his desire is for me. (Song of Solomon 7:10 NASB)

While we often apply Song of Solomon to married love, it is also a beautiful picture of Christ and His bride. I am so thankful to be Steve's beloved, but I am also overwhelmingly loved by Jesus. While Steve's physical presence in my Hallmark holidays may change, the presence of the One who loves me more than anything or anyone will never change. It will *never* change—and that truth will be as real as I choose to let it be. Every other sort of love is a risky he-loves-me-he-loves-me-not proposition (maybe that's what makes it such an emotional rush), but the love of God is failproof and foolproof. It's hard for me to get my mind around the fact that He doesn't just love me—like I say I love watermelon Jelly Bellys and the color orange—His desire is *for me*. He longs to be with me. Can you get your arms around how beautiful this relationship is?

The apostle Paul knew that our understanding of the size and scope of God's love was absolutely essential to everything else.

And I pray that you, being rooted and established in

love, may have power, together with all the Lord's holy people, to grasp how wide and long and high and deep is the love of Christ, and to know this love that surpasses knowledge—that you may be filled to the measure of all the fullness of God. (Ephesians 3:17–19 NIV)

This verse has come alive for me recently. I want to grasp the love of God from every dimension. I want to be able to comprehend it from my view from the top of the world or the bottom of the heap. I long to fully know His love when I'm surrounded by friends or alone in the card aisle, wishing for a time when hearts and flowers weren't so painful. It's into the cavern of my hurt and heartache that the full extent of His endless love can freely flow. When all other options are exhausted, I am uniquely positioned to be "filled to the measure of all the fullness of God." If we'll let them, I'm convinced that our emptiest days can create a conduit for our fullest full.

Our beautiful Immanuel has come so that we will never be the third wheel or the odd man out. His love brings hope and wholeness and belonging to our broken hearts. We can lean on Him on the holidays that hurt the most.

Finding Hidden Hope

Grab a blank sheet of paper and some colorful pens, and write out Song of Solomon 6:3, 7:10, and 8:5. Read these verses to yourself from the Lover of your soul . . . and choose to believe them.

. . . .

In a world where loving so often means losing, we give You our lives, our hope, and our shaky hearts. If love is an ocean, we move out beyond the shoreline and into the deep, where the only thing that can save us from love's ache is Love Himself. Amen.

nineteen

He Comes to Carry Our Government

For a child has been born—for us! . . . He'll take over the running of the world.

—Isaiah 9:6 MSG

I became a grandma for the first time in 2012, when our daughter gave birth to baby Grey. As you can imagine, I took one look at this baby and I was ruined. Simply put, I was crazy about him. His feet and hands and fingers were lovely and intricate and tiny. *All* of him was very tiny. And while we found him breathtaking, none of us would have trusted him with the running of the world. We wouldn't trust him with the running of the coffee pot. He's way too little—even two years later and bigger—and not at all qualified. The thought of it is absurd.

And yet Isaiah speaks prophetically of a child who would come to shoulder the weight of the government. He tells us that this child will bring restoration and peace in ever-increasing measure. No matter how outlandish the story may have sounded to Isaiah's listeners, it was true.

Jesus came through the womb of a woman to bear our burdens and right our world. Think about this for a moment: the pieces of your life that feel too heavy to carry or conquer are child's work for our King Jesus. I don't believe that He came to *remove* all those weights from our lives, but I know for certain that He came to lift them onto His shoulder so that we would never have to hold them alone. He came wrapped in the perfection of a baby but with the muscles of a superhero, ready to redeem and rescue.

> Jesus came to bring the not-yet to our right now, to take our frail and fractured attempts at controlling our own destiny onto His shoulder.

Fast-forward to the sixth chapter of Matthew's gospel. Here we find Jesus teaching His disciples how to pray. First He instructs them on how to address God, the Father. Next Jesus explains how to make a request. The first thing He tells them to ask for takes us right back to Isaiah's theme of government:

> "Your kingdom come, your will be done, on earth as it is in heaven." (Matthew 6:10 NIV)

Isaiah and Jesus both make it very clear: the government of heaven is very different and so much better than the one we've cobbled together here on earth. Isn't that great news? We are citizens of a new and better kingdom, and Jesus came so we could invite that kingdom into our lives. He came to bring the not-yet to our right now, to take our frail and fractured attempts at controlling our own destiny onto His shoulder.

At this time of year, when we honor the presidents who have shouldered the government of our nation, I am thankful we have a higher Ruler in authority. I don't know what battles you are facing this season or what burdens those battles have loaded on your shoulders, but I do know that the season will be short on joy if you try to carry those burdens all by yourself. Sometimes we make such a mess of the government of our own lives that we think maybe we need to fix it up before coming to Him for help. We pull out our duct tape and superglue and hope that Jesus can't see through the cracks to the mess inside. But the beautiful thing is that He already knows how unqualified we are to repair ourselves, so He doesn't ask us to. In fact, He came to take over the job. He came to restore our right to rest beneath His wing.

Today is a good day to invite the Child who was born for us to also *rule* for us, fight for us, and win for us.

Finding Hidden Hope

Take two minutes today, kneel in front of Him, and pray this one sentence from the depths of your heart: "Your kingdom come today . . . into my life, my battle, and my year." Then say it again and as many times as it takes to feel the weight shift from your shoulders to His.

. . . .

God of land and sea, creation and cosmos, be the God of my government today. Take control of my world, and carry the things too heavy for my weak arms and wobbly knees. Bring Your strength to my weakness, Your order to my chaos, and Your beauty to my battle. In the name of the Child—Your Child—born for us, amen.

twenty

Deep Thaw

He has made everything beautiful in its time.

—Ecclesiastes 3:11 NIV

Here in my mountain town, winter is all about weather. The snow usually starts in October, and we hope, for the sake of our ski resort–dependent economy, that Mt. Bachelor's slopes are open for business by Thanksgiving weekend. Most of us in Bend, Oregon, welcome the snow. Otherwise we would have chosen homes in Florida. I like to think we're sturdy folk.

However, even the hardiest winter people have limits. The snow that provided the no filter Norman Rockwell backdrop for the Christmas card photo does not feel as darling in April. Waking to a fresh fall of the white stuff is not very charming when it's covering freshly blooming tulips. Snow is beautiful and can be cozy, but when you're ready for spring, it's mostly annoying.

Have you ever felt like winter outstayed its welcome? Sometimes it seems life gets stuck in the sort of deep freeze described by C. S. Lewis as "always winter but never Christmas." I remember the day I found myself slipping around on my driveway, trying to dig my car out alone, fighting back memories of how my husband had always done the shoveling before he was sick, working to silence the pain of the changes of life caused by our battle, and finally just collapsing in a heap on the front seat of my frozen car. "It's too much for me," I told God. "It's too much winter in my life, and it feels like it's never going to thaw."

> These seasons are interwoven with His plan to create something bigger than our eyes can see or our hearts can imagine.

The undeniable truth about a season of pain and loss is that it makes everything feel cold and dormant. When sorrow surrounds us, even a sunny day has a sharp chill. While we long for the big thaw to come to our hearts and for spring to arrive with new hope and new life, Psalm 147 provides a blanket for these still-too-snowy nights:

> He sends His command throughout the earth; His word runs swiftly. He spreads snow like wool; He scatters frost like ashes; He throws His hailstones like crumbs. Who can withstand His cold? (vv. 15–17)

Well, that's not really very encouraging, is it? The psalmist paints a picture of a snow-throwing God. Here is God, wrangling the weather and tipping the thermostat downward in my life while I'm begging Him to send me to Florida or Texas or Tahiti—to send me anywhere but winter because I'm over being cold. Thankfully the psalm goes on:

> He sends His word and melts them; He unleashes His winds, and the waters flow. (v. 18)

Our brilliant creator, God, is the keeper of the seasons. He alone understands how important and interconnected they are in the grand scheme of life. Because of that, we can be certain that even in the middle of the longest winter, His word *will* come. It will melt the icy fragments of hope and cause them to water the earth beneath our feet. Here's more evidence, straight out of the Bible, which for our purposes today might also be called *The Big Book of Weather*:

> "As the rain and the snow come down from heaven, and do not return to it without watering the earth and making it bud and flourish, so that it yields seed for the sower and bread for the eater, so is my word that goes out from my mouth. It will not return to me empty, but will accomplish what I desire and achieve the purpose for which I sent it." (Isaiah 55:10–11 NIV)

Read the last line again, out loud, because it's too beautiful to miss. These seasons are part of His purpose. They are interwoven with His plan to create something bigger than our eyes can see or our hearts can imagine. The snow I hate in March becomes the water that prepares my backyard for my Fourth of July picnic. The blazing sun of August grows the crops that provide the wheat for the bread we eat with our Thanksgiving turkey.

When I'm standing on the green grass of summer, I rarely remember to thank God for those slushy mornings in April that created the lush lawn beneath my feet. But they are inextricably connected, and so are the seasons of my life. The battles I fought in 1999 helped prepare the blessings of 2009. The battles of 2014 are preparing something beautiful beneath the surface, something I may see in 2020 or on the other side of eternity, but His promise to me is this: the weather will not be wasted. His word *will* come, and it will accomplish His purposes in me. It's true for you too.

Finding Hidden Hope

Write a weather forecast in your journal. What season do you feel you are in right now? Now list a few things that might be happening beneath the surface of this season that will grow something beautiful down the road.

. . . .

Here is my heart today, God of my season. It is cold, maybe even frozen against feeling. Send Your Word to accomplish a beautiful, bountiful harvest. I wait for You. I trust You. I rest in You. In the name of the One who sees beginning to end, amen.

twenty-one

Springing Forward

"Look, I am about to do something new; even now it is coming.
Do you not see it? Indeed, I will make a way in the wilderness,
rivers in the desert . . . to give drink to My chosen people."

—Isaiah 43:19–20

Will you read the verse above out loud and listen to it burst with spring? It speaks of life so new and dynamic, it's bubbling up through desert ground. The season of spring feels forward-moving to me. The clocks move forward. The leaves move forward on their limbs. Blossoms move upward through newly softened soil. So much possibility exists in spring, but I've discovered that one thing is quite consistent with people in a season of pain or loss: it can be very difficult to embrace the unknown.

Those who find themselves in a fierce fight of nearly any kind know what it's like to be on the receiving end of very bad news. A phone call from a doctor. A letter from a spouse. A conversation with an employer. These are the moments that sock you in the gut and suck the wind from your lungs and teach you that surprises are often bad news.

The most brutal battles typically involve the one-two punch of shock and sadness so intense that it can, if we let it, redefine our expectations about all future "suddenlies." It's hard to trust that "something new" could be something good and easy to shield ourselves against the possibility of disappointment by taking shelter in what's old and familiar.

But this verse is certain in its assurance that the new thing God is doing is a good thing. What is this new thing? Isaiah tells us it's a new way through an old wilderness. I love that.

> *If you find yourself stuck in the cold winter of skepticism, wondering if God ever could or would do a new, good thing in your life, it's time to pray for spring.*

We need solid roads on which to travel. We need God's clear direction and protection as we move through desert land. This is that! This is the promise—that He will make your traveling smooth as you move to the next place. And along the way, He will provide water.

Since our battle began, God has been creating exactly this kind of spring in my life. He has been teaching me a new way of compassion by helping me launch an ALS wives support group. He has been teaching me a new way of generosity with our finances that has led to fresh life and joy. Time management has always been a struggle for me, but God has graciously given me new ways and systems that have led to multiplied effectiveness in every area. Turns out, I didn't need more time; I needed a new way with time. I didn't need more money; I needed a new way with it. And His ways are brilliant because they work.

If you find yourself stuck in the cold winter of skepticism, wondering if God ever could or would do a new, good thing in your life, it's time to pray for spring. When you set your clock ahead, let it be your commitment to trust the God who goes before you to make a new way for you, both on and off your battlefield. Even now it springs forth—and that might make this the best spring ever.

Finding Hidden Hope

For a full minute, sit and listen to the tick-tock of a clock. Each second is leading to spring, to life, to hope. Dare to believe that something new and good is on its way

. . . .

O God of my coming and going, I give You my way and my wandering, my desert and my desperation. Though it feels risky and dangerous, I'm asking You for something new. I trust Your goodness and grace to build a road out of this winter wilderness and into a fresh, bursting-with-life spring.

twenty-two

Springing Forward (Part 2)

*"Do not remember the past events, pay no attention
to the things of old. Look, I am about to do something
new; even now it is coming. Do you not see it? Indeed,
I will make a way in the wilderness, rivers in the
desert . . . to give drink to My chosen people."*

—Isaiah 43:18–20

Yesterday we talked about being brave enough to think forward, to believe that the new thing will be a good thing. Sometimes I think the thing that keeps us from moving ahead in our thinking is a reluctance to let go of what lies behind. We are good at replaying our past failures and mistakes and letting our dreams suffocate beneath the thumb of our personal regrets. However, it's equally dangerous to hold on to the past glory days.

In this very powerful verse, Isaiah admonishes the people to "forget the former things!" (43:18 NIV). If we move back a few verses, we'll see exactly what kinds of former things he's talking about.

This is what the LORD says—who makes a way in the sea, and a path through surging waters, who brings out the chariot and horse, the army and the mighty one together (they lie down, they do not rise again; they are extinguished, quenched like a wick). (vv. 16–17)

Isaiah is clearly referring to the exodus, when God parted the waters of the Red Sea and the Israelites passed through on dry ground while the Egyptian chariots and horses were drowned in its depths (Exodus 14). This is not just an event in Israel's history; it's one of her most significant national triumphs. It's the fourth down, fourth-quarter Super Bowl win. This is the story the Hebrews told their children when they tucked them into bed at night and wanted to reassure them that God was sovereign and good. And Isaiah says . . . forget it. Stop talking about it! That amazing victory is old news, and God is bringing newer, better news.

I've discovered this in my life: I can hold on to the old way, or I can grab on to the new way. But I can't do both any more than a trapeze artist can hold on to one bar while also taking a leap of faith to the next one. In order to grab the new thing, we often have to let go of the old one. And letting go is hard. Even when the thing we're clinging to isn't all that awesome, it's at the very least a known entity. And sometimes the known and visible is a safer bet than the unseen and unknowable. But the Bible is clear: the past will hold us back if we're not aggressive about moving forward into the new and now.

Paul said this:

Not that I have already obtained all this, or have already arrived at my goal, but I press on to take hold of that for which Christ Jesus took hold of me. Brothers and sisters, I do not consider myself yet to have taken hold of it. But one thing I do: Forgetting what is behind and straining toward what is ahead, I press on toward the goal to win the prize for which God has called me heavenward in Christ Jesus. (Philippians 3:12–14 NIV)

Paul's words are filled with action words. *Press. Take hold. Forget. Strain. Press* (again!). *Win.* It looks to me like this new way of thinking and moving forward doesn't just happen to us; we have to be willing to push toward it. To press away the memories of wins and wounds, triumphs and tragedies that so easily define and distract us. To dare to dream about a new way of thinking and a new season filled with new success and new scars.

It's hard to let go of the old. And the only thing that really makes it worth it is the fact that we know Jesus will be in the new season just like He was in the old one. He comes to bring a new thing and a new way. Are you ready for it? Spring is coming, and new dreams are coming with it.

Finding Hidden Hope

Take a look around today, looking for spring blossoms that may be pushing their way through winter's ground. Write a paragraph or two in your journal about any similarities between your current season and those resilient blooms.

. . . .

O God of the new thing, I often don't know whether to hold on or let go. Teach me to hear You, to obey You, and to trust You with what has been and what is coming. Give me courage to move into uncharted territory with fierce faith, knowing that You are with me. Amen.

twenty-three

Easter Words

The tongue has the power of life and death,
and those who love it will eat its fruit.

—Proverbs 18:21 NIV

When I was about ten years old, some girls at a mall made fun of the outfit I was wearing. I didn't know them, so I had no idea whether they were more refined fashionistas than I was (but trust me, they were—*everyone* was). Even though there was no clear reason to take their opinion seriously, I still went home and cried.

Many years later, as I was stopped at a red light, I heard a noise and saw something land on my windshield. Then something else. Substance? Saliva. Lots and lots of saliva. I cautiously turned to the left and looked straight into the eyes of a sneering man in a cargo van. He looked right back, smiled, and . . . spit at me again. I didn't know him (though I suspect he was probably married to one of the girls from the mall), so there was no emotional investment, and yet as I drove away, I cried. And it wasn't pretty, quiet, ladylike crying. Something in me just burst, and I was crying for every time I had been the weak one. The butt of the joke.

The loser. I cried years of tears stored up from the mall to that moment, trapped next to a bad guy at a red light.

So many battles in our lives are launched by an act of rejection, and that rejection is usually packaged up in potent little bundles of words. Whoever said sticks and stones were more damaging than words must not have spent much time in middle school. Or divorce court. Proverbs says words contain the power of life and death (18:21). James compares the damage done by our words to the way a fire ravages a forest (3:5–6).

> *Words may have the power to hurt us, but they cannot steal our life or breath or hope.*

As we look toward Easter, we could focus on many horrific aspects of the crucifixion. But here is the one that feels most tender to me today:

> The men in charge of Jesus began poking fun at him, slapping him around. They put a blindfold on him and taunted, "Who hit you that time?" They were having a grand time with him. (Luke 22:64 MSG)

I've read right over the top of this verse so many times, never taking a moment to absorb its impact. Jesus was not just pierced by the crown and the nails but by the sharp edge of slanderous words. He knows what it's like to be broken by insult, mocked by those who don't know Him, and denied by those who do. Jesus, the Word, became flesh and then took upon Himself all the words I would ever hear. The words that would mock and mark me. The words that would duke it out to decide my identity. He stood there that long night, while all His friends ran fast and far, and absorbed my rejection into His big heart. The really good news is this: Jesus didn't subject Himself to soul-crushing rejection just so He could empathize with us; He did it so He could heal us.

Yes, Proverbs says that words hold the power of death and life. But 1 Corinthians 15:55 says that the cross took the sting *out* of death. Words may have the power to hurt us, but they cannot steal our life or breath or hope. They cannot make us the loser. If you are bent beneath the weight of careless or cruel words spoken to or about you, know that Jesus came to heal your heart and restore your hope. He came to teach us a new way with words, bringing resurrection life where death once danced. His words always win, always heal, always bless. It's part of the promise of Easter.

Finding Hidden Hope

There are so many beautiful words in our language: *love, life, hope, healing, beauty, peace, harmony, joy, flourish, faithful, delight, strength,* and *tranquility,* just to name a few. Write down the five most beautiful words you can think of (or pick from my list). Now write them into sentences that describe the events of Easter and all it accomplished for us.

. . . .

Great God, You speak and our hearts are sparked with hope. Your Word sets life into motion and forms beauty from the ashes of rejection. May we know more than ever the language of heaven so we may speak it to a broken world. In the name of the Word made Flesh, amen.

twenty-four

Easter Healing

While he was still speaking a crowd came up, and the man who was called Judas, one of the Twelve, was leading them. He approached Jesus to kiss him, but Jesus asked him, "Judas, are you betraying the Son of Man with a kiss?" When Jesus' followers saw what was going to happen, they said, "Lord, should we strike with our swords?" And one of them struck the servant of the high priest, cutting off his right ear. But Jesus answered, "No more of this!" And he touched the man's ear and healed him.

—*Luke 22:47–51 NIV*

Oh, this is an action-packed passage, and it tells us about two distinct events that occurred almost simultaneously, each one significant and stunning, each applicable to the battles we face. First we see the arrest that would lead to the crucifixion of Jesus set into motion with a kiss. Judas, a man who walked and talked with Jesus for three years, a man who saw the signs and knew the miracles and enjoyed His friendship, was still willing to betray Him. So sad. If anyone you love has ever hurt you, ever wronged you, ever lied about you, then you know a bit of what Jesus must have been feeling as His dear friend sold Him to an angry mob of soldiers for a pocketful of cash. It's heart-wrenching and enough in itself to make this a terrible night in the life of a young servant living in a hostile world, so far from home.

The second big moment tumbles in on top of the first—as passionate, young Peter uses his sword to stop the progress of the plan of God (I totally see myself here, weapon in hand, swinging wildly at the very thing that will eventually set me free). This is not in alignment with God's purposes, so Jesus simply . . . fixes it.

This story is amazing. Think about it. Think of the just-knifed-in-the-back Jesus holding a bloody ear in His hand while the soldier screams in pain. Even in the midst of His own soul-deep agony, Jesus remembers this: He came to heal. So many times I get caught in the turmoil of the moment and forget why I'm really here. But Jesus doesn't. As He's about to die for humanity, it would have been the worst kind of hypocrisy to let this young man leave the garden broken and marked for the rest of his life by the events of Jesus' death. And so, in one beautiful motion, Jesus heals both His enemy's wound and Peter's mistake.

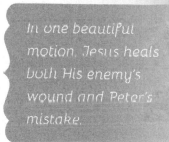

In one beautiful motion, Jesus heals both His enemy's wound and Peter's mistake.

Are you feeling broken by betrayal today? Stuck in anger or unforgiveness? Beyond the bunnies and brunches, Easter is about the healing and forgiveness that is ours because of Jesus. Healing was—and is—an extravagant benefit of the cross. His stripes for our sickness. His wounds for our weakness. Every mark that landed on His body that day was filled with power and purpose. Every bruise on the sinless skin of the Lamb of God contained freedom from death and disease and despair and healing for every betrayer's kiss. Every one. For everyone. Oh, how I love the cross!

Finding Hidden Hope

Read the lyrics to the hymn "Joyful, Joyful, We Adore Thee," and let them become your own prayer to the risen, healing Lord of all.

....

God of healing, You know my feeble, fickle heart. You know my wandering thoughts. Fasten me to You. Fix me to Your side. And in Your presence, I will be healed. In the name of the One who forgave and forgives, amen.

twenty-five

Earnestly Remembering

I will remember the deeds of the LORD; yes, I will remember your miracles of long ago. I will consider all your works and meditate on all your mighty deeds.

—*Psalm 77:11–12 NIV*

On the night before His arrest, Jesus established a memorial with His disciples. Though His dear friends could not have known what the next day would bring, on that Passover night they received instruction on how they should remember and honor it in the future.

After taking the cup, he gave thanks and said, "Take this and divide it among you. For I tell you I will not drink again from the fruit of the vine until the kingdom of God comes."

And he took bread, gave thanks and broke it, and gave it to them, saying, "This is my body given for you; do this in remembrance of me."

In the same way, after the supper he took the cup,

saying, "This cup is the new covenant in my blood, which is poured out for you." (Luke 22:17–20 NIV)

Jesus could have waited until after His death to establish the sacrament of communion with His disciples. And it would have made sense. When they could look back through the lens of the three dark days, the empty tomb, and the finished work of the Son of God, wouldn't it be easier to understand the memorial? Being served the bread and cup by the nail-scarred hands of the risen Savior surely would have made the meaning of the Lord's Supper crystal clear. And yet Jesus chose to tell them about it *ahead of time*, when the story was still murky and the battle was still hot.

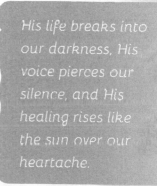

His life breaks into our darkness, His voice pierces our silence, and His healing rises like the sun over our heartache.

I hate uncertainty, and I definitely don't do my best thinking in the middle of it. I like to know what's coming and when. If I hear the voice of Jesus speak into my battle, I want it to answer questions rather than stir up more. But I've discovered that sometimes He just says, "Remember. Remember what I've already done. Remember who I am. Remember how I love you." And it's hard. It takes disciplined mind muscles to move away from the pain of the present and focus instead on the things God has already done and the victory He has promised.

One of the saddest books in the Bible contains one of

the most beautiful verses, and it shows us exactly how it's done:

> I remember my affliction and my wandering, the bitterness and the gall. I well remember them, and my soul is downcast within me. Yet this I call to mind and therefore I have hope: Because of the LORD's great love we are not consumed, for his compassions never fail. They are new every morning; great is your faithfulness. (Lamentations 3:19–23 NIV)

While experiencing affliction, the writer of Lamentations also latches on to a lifeline of hope by intentionally remembering the love of God, rich in mercy and flawlessly faithful. As humans we tend to forget what we should remember and remember what we should forget. Training our minds to automatically recall His goodness and love is a powerful resource in the middle of a fierce fight.

Countless times in the past three years, I have kept a white-knuckled grip on all I can remember about His character, His goodness, His track record in my life. I cling to the Friday promise like a life preserver, keeping my head above water until Sunday comes. Because it does. Sunday always comes. His life breaks into our darkness, His voice pierces our silence, and His healing rises like the sun over our heartache. But in between death and resurrection? He reminds us to remember.

What is the condition of your battle today? As we remember those who have fought for our country and our freedom, it's a good day to take a little time to focus again on the One who fought the ultimate battle to secure our eternity. Remember Him. Consider the ways He has met and led you in the past. Recall His promises for your future. Perhaps even set pen to paper, and write a memorial of all the things Jesus' death and resurrection here built into your life. As you view your life through the memorial of His goodness, you will find new strength and hope for all the seasons that lie ahead.

Finding Hidden Hope

Each time you eat or drink today, think of one thing God has done for which you are thankful. On a hard day, when it may be difficult to come up with a list, remember the cross.

....

God of my past, present, and future battles, I remember You today. I invite You to fill my mind with reasons to say thank You, helping me to create a memorial of hope. For all You are and all You have done—and most of all, for the gift of Your Son—my gratitude rolls on and on. Amen.

twenty-six

He Celebrates at Weddings

*On the third day a wedding took place in Cana of Galilee.
Jesus' mother was there, and Jesus and his disciples
had also been invited to the wedding as well.*

—John 2.1–2 NIV

The bride was a beauty. Perfect dress, perfect hair, perfect makeup. The weather had cooperated to create an impossibly romantic canopy of thunderclouds and shimmering sun for their outdoor sanctuary. Everything was lovely and I was enjoying it so much. Until I wasn't.

Steve hadn't been feeling well enough to go, so it was one of my first weddings without him. I don't mind going most places alone, but weddings are a whole different animal. Weddings are made for romance, and nothing could be less romantic than sitting alone at a reception table full of couples. I did okay until the time came for the dad to escort his daughter down the aisle. Just before beginning their epic walk, he gave her this look that was full of something so much more than love—it was adoration and pride with a little bit of "I can't believe my two-year-old is getting married!" It was beautiful. And I was a mess. I couldn't identify everything happening inside me. I only knew I was coming undone. Grief, weighty and tumultuous as the stormy sky, took shape and wrapped suffocating arms around me till I thought I couldn't breathe. After trying to be very strong for a very long time, I was breaking beneath the weight of a thousand sparkling dream fragments, raining down around me.

> *Jesus multiplies the joy because His vision is fixed fully on the purpose of the day rather than on the pain.*

I'm happy to report that I survived the wedding. I sucked in the tears, took some deep breaths, and saved the full force of my breakdown for the car on the way home. But the truth is that weddings are hard for me, and I don't think I'm alone in that. Beyond the mediocre food and endless toasting, weddings tug on our emotions in many different ways. For some, they're the reminder of painful, broken vows. For others, they shine yet another glaring light on the way love seems to be passing them by. For me, it's the idea that my girls might have to experience that iconic father-daughter dance with their brother instead. It's ironic that one person's big day can highlight another person's deepest heartache, but that's the truth of it. It's the way life moves in seasons and cycles of sorrow and celebration, and it's not wrong. It's just real and raw.

Since that day, I've learned a trick for getting through weddings. It's not a fancy trick. In fact, it's just a three-word trick. I keep these three words in my emotional pocket, and they are quick medicine when I start to feel heartsick.

The three words: *Jesus blessed weddings*. He did. He went to weddings even though He'd never have one of His own. He went and celebrated, and He added to the party. If I had the theological underpinnings for it, I would suggest here that He probably *danced* at weddings. Jesus, Man of Sorrows, even invested His own supernatural resources and brought the wine to the party.

When I look at Jesus' life, I see Him giving happy support to happy people. He blesses the event. He multiplies the joy because His vision is fixed fully on the purpose of the day rather than on the pain. Perhaps my vision needs to increase beyond surviving weddings. Maybe I should be asking, "How can I add to the joy here?" Is it possible that if Jesus can take ordinary water and make it into wine to bless the guests around Him, He could take my heart full of sadness and turn it into something beautiful to bless the guests around me?

I'm not gonna lie: it takes a significant amount of spiritual muscle to pry my eyes off my own self and fix them on His purpose in sending me into a celebration I would rather not attend. But I'm telling you, every time I'm willing to do it, *He comes*. He comes to me, and I feel His love washing over pain and setting me free from the tyranny of sorrow, making fresh room for the restoration of joy.

Weddings are hard. But Jesus blesses them. I'm going to bless them too.

Finding Hidden Hope

Read Isaiah 62:5 out loud, and write a few sentences about what it means to you. How might a firm grasp on this verse help you face the days and occasions on which you feel alone?

. . . .

O God, rich in love, I bring You my weary heart. Give me eyes to see Your love for me, even when I feel on the fringes of the festivities. Set me free to rejoice with those who rejoice and to add life to the party. Lend me Your love for people and Your heart for the celebration. Amen.

Summer
and Fall

twenty-seven

He Holds Us Tightly

*The LORD your God, who is going before you, will fight
for you, as he did for you in Egypt, before your very
eyes, and in the wilderness. There you saw how the
LORD your God carried you, as a father carries his son,
all the way you went until you reached this place.*

—Deuteronomy 1:30–31 NIV

Like most churches in America, ours honors the dads on
Father's Day every year. And each time the dads stand
as we thank them with our applause, I look around, trying to
mentally capture the father-child stories in the faces:

- One dad raising his two girls alone, feeling pretty
  desperate most of the time.
- One dad whose ex-wife got custody of their three
  children and then moved two states away. He pays
  child support regularly but sees them rarely.
- A dad who buried his sweet daughter this year, and
  he misses her with every single breath.
- A girl who buried her dad this year, and her life is
  more peaceful because of it.

- Another whose dad went to prison, and she suspects some people would have rather he died.
- And a dad whose wife miscarried their first child, and he's just not sure whether to stand or not.

When I look at my own kids, I wonder: How will they feel on the Father's Days to come? What will they believe about how they have been loved and protected and treasured? Whether or not we realize it, so many of our feelings about the love of our heavenly Father are shaped by the way we felt about our earthly father. Though no man was built to measure up to the care and love offered by an endlessly faithful God, the associations are impossible to avoid altogether.

> *God is a good Father. And good fathers fight for their children.*

As I talk with people going through difficult battles, I find that some are becoming more beautiful than they have ever been, while others are becoming more bitter, isolated, and cynical. As I dig more deeply into their history and heartache, I've discovered that the main variable in which kind of person they become is whether or not they really know and trust God as their Father. Jesus also talked about how important it is that we see God as trustworthy:

"Which of you fathers, if your son asks for a fish, will give him a snake instead? Or if he asks for an egg, will give him a scorpion? If you then, though you are evil, know how to give good gifts to your children, how much more will your Father in heaven give the Holy Spirit to those who ask him!" (Luke 11:11–13 NIV)

Though it may seem elementary, I want to restate it, because our belief in this concept is essential to every battle we will ever face: God is a good Father. And good fathers fight for their children. They protect, provide, and invest. They love unconditionally. They go to bat for the kids they love. Not all fathers do these things because not all fathers are good. But God is a good, good Father. He is, in fact, the best Father, and He loves us with the best kind of love.

Just two chapters later in the Gospel of Luke, Jesus tells us the story of a really good dad in a really difficult situation. But it's not just a story; it's a word picture meant to point our hearts toward home and toward the outrageous love of our excellent Abba. Imagine the scene: A beloved son has cashed in his inheritance, leveraged his father's legacy, and hit the road for greener pastures. The father is heartbroken. When the son comes to the end of himself, he takes a home among pigs and wishes for the life he once knew. The father is under no obligation to respond. The father, in fact, would probably be wise to give the son a little lesson in appreciation. A little humility would be good for a boy like that. Even the son expects to be treated as a slave; it's what he has coming. The dad in Jesus' story, however, has no such inclination.

"So he got up and went to his father. But while the son was still a long way off, his father saw him and was filled with compassion. He ran, threw his arms around his neck, and kissed him. The son said to him, 'Father, I have sinned against heaven and in your sight. I'm no longer worthy to be called your son.' But the father told his slaves, 'Quick! Bring out the best robe and put it on him; put a ring on his finger and sandals on his feet. Then bring the fattened calf and slaughter it, and let's celebrate with a feast, because this son of mine was dead and is alive again; he was lost and is found!'" (Luke 15:20–24)

Oh, do you see it there? It's right there in the words of Jesus, whom I'm guessing told this story with a wide smile, knowing the way His Father threw a party. Our Father is not just good; He's gracious, and He loves to welcome us home. In fact, He says the son was "dead and now he's alive." The season of my life is so intense right now that I am firmly, absolutely convinced: I'm as good as dead without the love of our Father. He is fighting for me, holding tightly to me, and even when my feet wander far from truth and hope, He runs to meet me and welcomes me back.

I don't know your father story. I only know you have one. And I know that no matter what you're facing today, you have a God who is ready and willing to fold you in His arms and let you rest in His embrace. He is a Dad worth celebrating.

Finding Hidden Hope

Make a list of all the good things a good dad does. Circle the things you believe are true of our heavenly Father, and underline the things you have trouble associating with His character. Read over your list prayerfully, asking God to show you any places in your heart that need a truth infusion about who He really is to you.

....

I am amazed and undone today by this truth: the Father of all is the Father of me. Your hands have led and fed me thus far. You have carried me when my legs were too weak to walk. You have kept me safe in the shadowy valley. I love You and take my place again in Your presence. Amen.

twenty-eight

He Declares Our Freedom

It is for freedom that Christ has set us free.

—*Galatians 5:1 NIV*

On July 2, 1776, John Adams and fifty-five others signed the Declaration of Independence. It was an explosive document, listing a long lineup of grievances and demanding the dissolution of the political bands connecting the thirteen colonies to the oppression of Great Britain and King George. Though some of the exact dates are in dispute, everyone agrees the signing of the Declaration was a supremely significant event.

Two days before setting pen to parchment, John Adams wrote to his wife, Abigail:

The second day of July, 1776, will be the most memorable epoch in the history of America. I am apt to believe that it will be celebrated by succeeding generations as the great anniversary festival. It ought to be commemorated as the day of deliverance, by solemn acts of devotion to God Almighty. It ought to be solemnized with pomp and parade, with shows, games, sports, guns, bells, bonfires, and illuminations, from one end of this continent to the other, from this time forward forever more.[3]

Mr. Adams may have missed the mark by two days, but his vision was spot-on. Independence Day has become our most important national holiday, the day we celebrate our freedom from the bonds of tyranny and injustice, complete with pomp and parade, food and fireworks. We call it America's birthday, but is it really? The signing of the Declaration of Independence did not purchase our freedom. It was the fight that followed. It was the Burning of Norfolk and the Battle of Blanford, the Siege of Fort Watson, and so many others like them. It was the blood poured out on the ground of the land we love by the soldiers and citizens who refused to settle for anything less than liberty. Our forefathers declared freedom well in advance. They could imagine the bonfires and the bells going off to celebrate what would come to be a beautiful reality: Land of Liberty. I'm convinced that this ability to envision the final outcome makes all the difference in the battles we fight for our own freedom.

In Luke 4, Jesus sits down in the temple, opens a scroll, and reads this divine declaration:

> "The Spirit of the Lord is on me, because he has anointed me to proclaim good news to the poor. He has sent me to proclaim freedom for the prisoners and recovery of sight for the blind, to set the oppressed free, to proclaim

the year of the Lord's favor." Then he rolled up the scroll, gave it back to the attendant and sat down. The eyes of everyone in the synagogue were fastened on him. He began by saying to them, "Today this scripture is fulfilled in your hearing." (4:18–21 NIV)

I wonder: When Jesus read that scripture, what did He see? Did He look ahead to the battle of the cross? Could He picture the moment He would defeat the powers and principalities constantly at work to keep us shut up and held down? And when I dig a little deeper, I wonder something more personal and tender. Is it possible, do you suppose, that as Jesus sat in that temple on a dusty day in Jerusalem, He could see . . . *me*? Did the Son of Man see ahead to the day when war would be declared on my family by a monster of a motor-neuron disease? Did He see the moment when we decided we would not become slaves to fear or bitterness or anger? And what if our great God could see the very second we determined to use our freedom to help free others? Wouldn't that just be something?

> The ability to envision the final outcome makes all the difference in the battles we fight for our own freedom.

What about your battle? Where is it headed? If there were freedom to be gained from the fights you are facing, what might it be? And let's brainstorm together for a moment to imagine how your freedom might open a window into someone else's prison cell. Wouldn't that just be something?

I dare you to dream it. In fact, friend, I dare you to declare it. Let's see what might happen if we are willing to believe that our battles are leading to greater freedom than we have ever known. Let's choose to believe that bells and bonfires are in our future because we serve the God who declared and secured our freedom, once and for all.

Finding Hidden Hope

Write out your own personal Declaration of Independence. Clearly list any tyrants in your life and describe how freedom might look in the weeks, months, and years to come.

. . . .

God of freedom, thank You for fighting the battle of the cross to break into my prison cell. Today I declare my independence from sin and shame and my complete dependence on You. Give me eyes of faith to see the land of liberty You are creating for me and will create through me as I follow Your lead. Amen.

twenty-nine

He Gives Us Rest

What a beautiful thing, God, to give thanks, to sing an anthem to you, the High God! To announce your love each daybreak, sing your faithful presence all through the night.

—Psalm 92:1–2 MSG

Day and night. Night and day. The rhythm of worship in the Psalms is almost hypnotically beautiful as it matches its cadence to nature. The older I get, the more I love the healthy ebb and flow of rising, working, resting, eating, sleeping. Sunrise and sunset give boundaries to the endless run of days into weeks, into months, into years. Morning marks a start, evening a finish, but each calls us to worship well.

I'm increasingly convinced that the movement of day into night is majestically ordained by our Creator for the purpose of soul health. We need both night and day to function effectively. A friend of mine lived in an Alaskan town where she experienced long seasons of either endless nighttime or midnight sun. I was surprised when she said that the constant darkness was difficult but that living in unending daylight was nearly impossible. She needed the settledness that came from an honest-to-goodness inky-black night-time. Without it, she found herself unable to rest and quiet her heart enough to refuel after a day of hard work.

In seasons of battle, we need the night and the quiet it brings. Though a land of perennial sunshine sounds good in theory, we are wired up to require respite from the full-throttle action of demanding days. Though I know I need this, actually *doing* it has required intentional decision making and a healthy dose of discipline. It's easy to fill life to the brim with people and going and moving and doing. It's especially tempting when solitude brings me face-to-face with the things in my life I wish were different. The tendency to try to drown out sorrow with constant activity is common in our world, where distractions are a dime a dozen.

> The tendency to try to drown out sorrow with constant activity is common in our world.

Several of my friends are single. They are anxious to find true love and sometimes feel they live on the battlefield of hope deferred, waiting for something that is always just out of reach. I've watched them choose different strategies for navigating their struggle, and while they all handle it differently, most of them take at least one spin through the land of frantic activity. They fill every moment with people, friends, parties, hoping to avoid any downtime when they might find themselves alone. And maybe that's the heart of it: if we view quiet time as lonely time, we'll be tempted to choose a life in the land of the midnight sun instead. But solitude is essential for success, and we know it because Jesus modeled it.

Before choosing His disciples, Jesus created a quiet night for Himself to pray.

> One of those days Jesus went out to a mountainside to pray, and spent the night praying to God. When morning came, he called his disciples to him and chose twelve of them, whom he also designated apostles. (Luke 6:12–13 NIV)

Solitude helps us make good decisions. Constant activity muddies our judgment. That's a compelling enough reason to cherish a little downtime, but here's another. In Matthew 14, we read of the execution of John the Baptist, Jesus' cousin and friend. Here is Jesus' response:

> When Jesus heard what had happened, he withdrew by boat privately to a solitary place. (v. 13 NIV)

In the face of suffering and loss, the Son of God needed time to get away and grieve, to be with His Father. The further I move into the heart of suffering, the more convinced I am that I need the same thing. I don't always want it. I'd much rather drown out the quiet, and convenient distractions are easy to find—they're usually as close as the nearest on/off switch. I'm finding, however, that those panaceas only numb pain. They can never heal it. Solitude helps us move out of the chaos of sorrow and into a place where

God's voice can be heard and can speak life to the hurting places. One more way we see Jesus use quiet time to His advantage is found in the same chapter in Matthew, as the crowds press in on Him:

> Immediately Jesus made the disciples get into the boat and go on ahead of him to the other side, while he dismissed the crowd. After he had dismissed them, he went up on a mountainside by himself to pray. (vv. 22–23 NIV)

Jesus needed solitude to help Him deal with the demands of success. It's easy to feel important and awesome when the crowds are shouting our name, but a few minutes in the presence of an almighty, omniscient Creator quickly remind us of our size and shape in His story. When I bring my big achievements to the quiet place of God's love and care, I reconnect with the Source of grace from which all winning flows. It's good to be reminded that I am unimaginably small but infinitely loved.

As you enter this season of long, hot days, determine to deal with the distractions that would keep you from practicing solitude. He is the God of night and day, and He longs to meet us in the dusky quiet and speak words of light and life. What He speaks in the dark will sustain us in the day and in all the battles the days may bring.

Finding Hidden Hope

Pick one day this week to experience the beauty of dawn and dusk. Take twenty minutes in the silvery twilight of early morning, and thank God for the day ahead. Later, find a quiet place as the sun sinks low, and record your thoughts from the day you just lived. Invite Him to speak into your battle and to meet you in all the nights and days ahead.

. . . .

O God of my coming and going, my rising and waking, my quiet and clamor, thank You for the gift of night and day. Show me the secrets of solitude, and give me the will to embrace its beauty in sorrow and success. For Your name's sake, amen.

thirty

He Keeps Good Time

Teach us to number our days, that we may gain a heart of wisdom.

—Psalm 90:12 NIV

When Steve was diagnosed with ALS, it was like hanging a two-to-five-year timer around his neck. The ticking was loud and conspicuous as we made plans for the unknown yet limited time we had left. We also knew that the process would cause many things to slowly expire: first was his ability to work full-time, then his golf game, then driving. At the time of this writing, we are preparing for a new challenge—tomorrow will be the day a feeding tube is placed, as eating has become more and more difficult. For Steve, the clock is always ticking on life as he knew it.

Sometimes I've wanted to stop the clock and absorb a moment of time so I don't lose it or forget it. Other times, quite honestly, watching the man I love suffer so much makes me want to fast-forward to a day when he is free from the ravages of disease. Slow down? Speed up? I don't always know what to do with time, but that's okay. The writer of Ecclesiastes assures us that the pendulum swings according to the will of God:

There is a time for everything,
and a season for every activity under the heavens:
a time to be born and a time to die,
a time to plant and a time to uproot,
a time to kill and a time to heal,
a time to tear down and a time to build,
a time to weep and a time to laugh,
a time to mourn and a time to dance. (3:1–4 NIV)

Though He lives in eternity, time is as real to God as it is to us. I'm convinced that He has been to every minute I will ever face, and none of them are outside His control. He is the God of the present, so I can trust Him with my very now. But He is also the God of the future, so I can trust Him with all the minutes that are to come. Look at where this beautiful passage goes next:

He has made everything beautiful in its time. He has also set eternity in the human heart; yet no one can fathom what God has done from beginning to end. (v. 11 NIV)

Read the first line of that last verse out loud. Notice that it's past perfect tense. He has already made everything beautiful . . . in its time. His beautiful work in us is a foregone conclusion, but the unfolding will happen over the course of time. And then we see an entirely new time frontier: *He has also set eternity in our hearts.* Not only is our gracious God doing something wonderful in the right-now time in which we live; He is also opening our eyes to the vast expanse of wonder that is to come. Eternity. No ticking timers. No dying muscles. No breaking hearts.

So how do we make peace with time while we're in a difficult season that seems endless? The apostle Paul offers an answer in 2 Corinthians, and these words are burned into barn wood, hanging on the wall of my office, where they remind me how to live as a citizen of the now-and-not-yet kingdom of God.

> Therefore we do not lose heart. Though outwardly we are wasting away, yet inwardly we are being renewed day by day. For our light and momentary troubles are achieving for us an eternal glory that far outweighs them all. So we fix our eyes not on what is seen, but on what is unseen, since what is seen is temporary, but what is unseen is eternal. (4:16–18 NIV)

The troubles on our timeline are temporary. They're real and they're painful, but they're temporary. And this verse promises that when our feet are firmly planted in forever, the pain of the past will seem like a blip on the screen or a tiny bobble in an otherwise endless sea of grace. As I live out the struggle of the day, I remember this one thing: God has put eternity in my heart. It lives there as a constant reminder of what's yet to come. I'm so thankful for the promise that His purpose will outlive my pain, His love will outlast my longing, and His celebration will overwhelm my sorrow. We are sojourners here on this planet, but our minutes are adding up to something truly miraculous—the glorious unfolding of the redemption story of God. I can hardly wait.

Finding Hidden Hope

Close your eyes, and take ten long, deep breaths, letting your mind drift toward the idea of heaven. Imagine what it might look like, how it might feel being that close to the glory of God and in right relationship with His people. You are able to imagine a place you've never been and feelings you've never experienced because God has put eternity in your heart. He is preparing all of us for something more beautiful than our ten deep breaths could ever conjure up, and this is the best news of all.

....

God of all my minutes, You are the conductor of my days and the joy of my life. You have placed eternity in my heart, where it pulses with the hope of all that is yet to be. I give You my now and my not yet, and I trust You with all the beauty that will unfold in time. Amen.

thirty-one

Facing Change

"Look! I am making all things new."

—*Revelation 21:5 NET*

I have always loved fall. In the Cascade Mountains where I live, it marks the arrival of boots and scarves and school supplies. It signals the end of some things but the beginning of things I like better, which is really what we want a season change to be, isn't it? Yes, we want new. But new in all good ways. Sometimes, however, a new season is not good news.

When our feet landed on the battlefield of ALS, my favorite season took a turn toward the ominous. For the first time, I didn't want the changes it was bringing, and I felt myself digging my heels into September. I remember the day I took a walk through a park and watched a mini tornado of leaves, loosened from their limbs by a gust of wind. They circled, spun in a riot of gold and red and orange, creating a color storm as they fell. I could almost imagine that they were racing each other to welcome the changing of the seasons.

I wished I was like that. I wanted so badly to be one who could gracefully let go of the branch and fly fast and free, trusting the God who was good in the old to be every bit as good in the new.

But that's not me. I am not the leaf that happily floats because the wind says she should. I am one who clings to the security of the season that was. In fact, I look at the leaves that strap themselves in and dare the wind to break their hold, and I admire their pluck, all the while knowing that they are silly to resist the pull of the seasons. They will look ridiculous up there, covered in snow. When summer comes, and green is the new orange, their rusty coats will be hopelessly outdated . . . so *last year*. When it's time to let go, it's time to let go. Move on. It makes so much sense, but why is it so hard?

The apostle John wrote to people like me. People clinging desperately to the only solid thing beneath their fingers, even if its strength is an illusion. Wanting to jump, afraid to jump. Wanting to stay, afraid to stay. In fact, pause here and think of the thing you would most like to cling to right now. Perhaps it's a relationship or a bank account or a job or a calling. Now read these words out loud so your ears can hear them fall like rain into your season:

Then I saw "a new heaven and a new earth," for the first heaven and the first earth had passed away, and there was no longer any sea. I saw the Holy City, the new Jerusalem, coming down out of heaven from God, prepared as a bride beautifully dressed for her husband. And I heard a loud voice from the throne saying, "Look! God's dwelling place is now among the people, and he will dwell with them. They will be his people, and God himself will be with them and be their God. 'He will wipe every tear from their eyes. There will be no more death' or mourning or crying or pain, for the old order of things has passed away." (Revelation 21:1–4 NIV)

Our world is in a state of constant decay, but the mission of God has always been the restoration and renewal of all things, including you and me. Because He is a creative genius, *new* is not a passing fancy with Him; it's His very character. The always-redemptive purpose of God elbows its way into dead and dying situations to create abundant possibilities and multiplied beginnings. It's so much easier to let go of the old when we are certain He is creating something good in the new. This certainty gives us courage to face the changes with grace. And you *can* be certain, you know. Jesus came to create. He came to restore, reform, and conform us to His own image. As we let Jesus do His work, we can trust that the work will be good and that we don't have to brace ourselves for change.

This is the part where I wish I could promise you that all the good, reforming things God has planned in the next season of your life will *feel* good. But I can't. I can only promise that they will *be* good and that they will *create* good in your life if you determine to cling only to Him.

Finding Hidden Hope

Read the verses from Revelation 21 out loud whenever your heart is tempted to fear the new season or when you feel desperate for a new season to arrive.

. . . .

Today I bring You the spinning seasons and changing colors of my life. I release my white-knuckled grip on "the way it's always been" and ask that, in Your goodness, You would do something better than all my dreams. Give me courage to trust You with joy. In the name of the One who does not change but does bring change, amen.

thirty-two

The Tears That Grow the Harvest

*Restore our fortunes, Lord, as streams renew the
desert. Those who plant in tears will harvest with
shouts of joy. They weep as they go to plant their seed,
but they sing as they return with the harvest.*

—*Psalm 126:4–6 NLT*

When I was in high school, I spent two summers on my
sister's farm in Montana. I loved Big Sky country and
farm life because the whole community was engaged in
the risks and rewards inherent in trying to make a living
off the land. Discussing the weather in Montana during
harvest is not small talk. It's vital. They need rain, but not
too much rain. Sun, but not too much sun. And please, dear
God, no hail.

My sister and her husband lived in a region notorious
for its hailstorms. Often they hit without warning and
seemed almost vindictive in the way they moved through the
area, devastating some fields and skipping others entirely.
Some farmers believed in insuring themselves against the

possibility of hail, and some did not. Consequently, though everyone hoped and prayed and worked for a bountiful harvest, not everyone experienced one. Every year, it seemed, harvest stirred different emotions in different people.

I've never farmed a piece of land myself, but I've certainly felt like the hailed-out farmer before. Have you ever mourned the devastation of your own land while watching someone else haul in a bumper crop? Jeremiah must have felt the same way, because he tossed out this terse question to the Lord:

> *Have you ever mourned the devastation of your own land while watching someone else haul in a bumper crop?*

> Yet let me plead and reason the case with You: Why does the way of the wicked prosper? Why are all they at ease and thriving who deal very treacherously and deceitfully? (Jeremiah 12:1 AMP)

It's one thing when we feel we've been overlooked by a friend or family member, but it's another altogether when we feel disregarded by God Himself. Overlooked. Hailed out. Sometimes we avoid these questions, feeling they're too dangerous to ask, but Jeremiah didn't shy away from the tough stuff. I like that. It opens up new realms of authenticity in my own relationship with God when I see that Jeremiah got away with it.

And so I've asked, *Why Steve, who has worked hard and*

served You all his life? Why the man I love, while his children are young and still need a dad? Why me, when I've given my life to Your kingdom and worked really hard to be the good girl I think You want me to be? Oh, believe me, I've asked. And Jesus, in His faithfulness, has answered in ways that leave no room for doubt. He has convinced me of His passionate care and love—in the presence of our enemies and in the absence of a visible bumper crop.

The truth is, God doesn't overlook us. Any of us. He knows each hair on our heads and each thought in our minds and each word that does or doesn't make it out of our mouths. He knows and cares, like a mother cares for her new baby. He cares, like a husband cares for his darling wife. But His caring does not keep us from all battle. In fact, in His goodness, He walks with us into battle and helps us find the beauty buried there.

In the past three years, I have learned that one of the sneakiest thieves of my joy and freedom is comparison. When I look at someone else's success or good fortune or health as the enemy of my own, then I am on the fast track to inconsolable misery. God is *for* me and *with* me, and His love does not leave me stranded or alone, no matter how much I may feel it when I view someone else's big win. I can be certain that my win is on the way because He is good and just and He will not be in debt to me. I will plant with all my heart because I know that my harvest is coming and that I will haul those sheaves in with rejoicing.

Finding Hidden Hope

Think of a time when you have questioned the equal distribution of God's blessings. Now think of everyone you know who has less than you have. Take a moment to thank Him for His gifts in your life and to ask Him for what you need.

....

Lord of the harvest, I step beneath Your rainfall of grace. Neither withering hail nor winsome sun can separate me from Your love. Bless this battleground, watered with tears. May it yield a harvest of hope for a hungry world. Amen

thirty-three

The Days That Mark Us

We are hard pressed on every side, but not crushed;
perplexed, but not in despair; persecuted, but not
abandoned; struck down, but not destroyed.

—2 Corinthians 4:8–9 NIV

I believe that all holidays serve as mileposts—we use them to mark the movement in our lives. We compare the pictures of the kids around the Christmas tree each year; we mark who's around the Thanksgiving table this year and who is missing. Without seasons and holidays, the calendar would be an endless highway of days with no mileposts. One of the most recent mileposts in our country is September 11, 2001. I've not met a single adult who cannot pinpoint exactly where they were at the time the planes crashed into buildings and it seemed our nation was crumbling down around us.

September 11, 2001, marked a moment in our history. The event was loaded with fear, grief, anger, heroism, and national pride. I'm certain the terrorists considered how much the pain they inflicted on America would hurt us, but I'm not sure they rightly measured how much it would inspire and motivate us. Pain does that. It marks us, yes, but it also moves us in one direction or another. We can't often control the pain we experience, but we do have some power over where that pain points us and how it shapes who we become.

I hate pain and I love pleasure. That's the truth of it. I used to secretly believe that excessive amounts of pain in the lives of believers meant they were doing something wrong. I'm not sure where I got this idea, because every significant Bible hero from Job to Jesus has a biography marked by heartache. Tales of abandonment, barrenness, persecution, family betrayal, murder, corruption, and martyrdom run through nearly every page of the holy canon, reminding us that life in this fallen world is short, hard, and seriously unfair . . . but God is good. And in His goodness, He often chooses not to shield us from all pain but to use it to make us into the heroes He alone knows we can become. So how do we do it? What makes the difference between those who grow and those who give up?

One answer is found in Paul's letter to the Romans. He writes to them near the end of his ministry, after having experienced more than a lifetime's worth of pain (see 2 Corinthians 11:24–26 if you'd like to compare affliction lists with him). Paul lays out a brilliant theology for pain management in the whole chapter, but he comes to a stunning conclusion in the very last verses:

> No, in all these things we are more than conquerors through him who loved us. For I am convinced that

neither death nor life, neither angels nor demons, neither the present nor the future, nor any powers, neither
height nor depth, nor anything else in all creation, will
be able to separate us from the love of God that is in
Christ Jesus our Lord. (Romans 8:37–39 NIV)

Can you feel the jostling going on here? Circumstances,
situations, and the very powers of heaven and hell are all
pushing and pulling, working to move us either toward or
away from the God who loves us. If Paul's summation is
that, in spite of their best efforts, none of these things can
possibly separate us from the love of God, that leads me
to wonder: What could? Because I know plenty of people
who have experienced pain and it moved them far from
faith. I think the thing most likely—and maybe the only
thing with the capability—to shipwreck my faith is me.
When I run into a day that marks me with an ugly scar, I
have to determine whether I will let it cause me to question the love of God for my life or not. I have the ability to
choose to let the mark call out the hero in me and move
me to a place of greater trust in God's character and deeper
commitment to His purposes. I can decide, in fact, that the
very thing the enemy meant to destroy me will instead
inspire me to regroup and rebuild stronger than I was
before. I will not let the terrorists win the day because I
am more deeply rooted in His love than I was before my
world caved in.

On one of our dark days with ALS, I sat down and wrote
this verse out in my own words so that it told my own story.

No, in spite of how this day turned out, we are still winning because our lives are marked by His love. For I am unshakably convinced that neither life nor death, nor ALS, nor feeding tubes, nor scary decisions, nor things in this day or things in tomorrow or all the tomorrows to come, will be able to disillusion or distance us from the love of God, poured out for us through the blood of His Son, Jesus. (author's paraphrase)

So much about who we become is determined on the painful days. How we let suffering mark and move us will be either a gift or a curse, a tragedy or a triumph. If you decide today to lean into the pain and let it push you deep into the love of God, I feel certain you will emerge from your battle more beautiful than you have ever been. And that's how heroes are made.

Finding Hidden Hope

Write your own version of Romans 8:37-39.

....

O God of the days that mark us, fasten me like glue to Your goodness. When fear and frustration work to pry me away from Your love, I have decided: I will not budge. I will not bend. I will not move. Because I know Your love is everything. In the name of Your Son who was marked with nails for my freedom, amen.

thirty-four

The God Who Sees

She gave this name to the LORD who spoke to her: "You are the God who sees me," for she said, "I have now seen the One who sees me."

—Genesis 16:13 NIV

On November 11, 1921, the United States laid to rest the remains of a World War I soldier, his name "known but to God." The Virginia burial site became known as the Tomb of the Unknown Soldier and symbolizes respect and dignity for the warriors whose bodies were not able to be identified—those who gave their lives in obscurity. November 11 is now called Veteran's Day.

The Tomb of the Unknown Soldier has always seemed very beautiful but very sad to me. Each of us longs to be seen and known. We want someone to witness our lives and know that we really did exist, that we really did matter. But in this push-and shove society, it's hard to be noticed and easy to feel invisible. That's why I love the story of Hagar.

Hagar is a mysterious and much-maligned character. As the maid to Abram and Sarai, it appears she had a quiet life until God promised the couple a son. Sarai, unable to trust Him to fulfill His promise through her own aging body, devised an alternate plan, and Hagar found herself swept into Abraham's bed and Sarai's faithless scheme. The maid goes along with the plan, but her attitude turns sour as soon as she gets pregnant. Considering the twisted dynamics of this domestic situation, it's not hard to imagine how her behavior might be justified. Did Hagar want to have Abraham's baby? Did she perhaps love another? Did she hope for children that belonged only to her and not to her mistress? So many possibilities for heartache here.

Sarai mistreats Hagar so viciously that it drives her away. This part of the story is heart-wrenching because it reveals how utterly alone Hagar is in the world. It seems her entire identity is tangled up in the house of Abraham, and now she is with child and without protection. She stumbles through the wilderness until an angel finds her and speaks into her broken heart, asking a provocative question, "Hagar, slave of Sarai, where have you come from and where are you going?"

Hagar, on the run and all alone, hears her very own name trip off the tongue of a heavenly being. Suddenly, the invisible woman is divinely seen. Known. Chosen. The angel gives her clear instruction and some important promises about her baby's future before sending her back home. Hagar's response is to give the Lord a new name, and I think it's one of the most beautiful names we find in the whole story of God. 'You are the God who sees me,' for she said, 'I have now seen the One who sees me.'"

The One who sees me. This aspect of God's nature may not be as important on a day when our banners are waving and the crowds are cheering. In the seasons when we feel celebrated and surrounded, God can easily become just another set of eyes in the bleachers. But when we're running for our lives or wandering through the wilderness of isolation, failure, or rejection, the discovery that God is watching is worth nearly everything.

David reiterates Hagar's heart in Psalm 139:

You have searched me, LORD, and you know me. You know when I sit and when I rise; you perceive my thoughts from afar. You discern my going out and my lying down; you are familiar with all my ways. Before a word is on my tongue you, LORD, know it completely. You hem me in behind and before, and you lay your hand upon me. Such knowledge is too wonderful for me, too lofty for me to attain. (vv. 1–6 NIV)

Even after following God for most of my life, I still wake up some mornings feeling invisible. If I'm honest, some days I *want* invisible. I want to hide away from everyone, including Him. I lick my wounds and curl up into my own pain, trying to lock out the sounds of all other voices. It's into those moments God speaks. He pursues me. He finds me and reminds me that my battle has not moved me outside His line of vision.

I have a big question for you today: Where have you come from and where are you going? Are you on the run from hurts and heartache? I promise you this: He sees you on your battlefield, and you will never be unknown. This is exactly the right time to let Him speak.

Finding Hidden Hope

Read Psalm 139:1–18 out loud, like you really mean it. Write a list of all the ways God sees and knows us.

....

Dear God of all, I confess that I am not hidden from You or shrouded in the darkness of my own shame or sadness. I open up my life to Your eyes. Search me, know me, break through the mists of confusion, and find me here, helpless without You but everything with You. I am Yours alone. Amen.

thirty-five

The Dance of Grief and Gratitude

*Enter his gates with thanksgiving and his courts with
praise; give thanks to him and praise his name.*

—Psalm 100:4 NIV

Deep in the heart of November, I received two e-mails
from women who were each fighting fierce battles,
one losing her husband to ALS, the other losing her husband to an addiction he seemed unable to control. Different
stories with similar shades of emotional trauma. I thought
about how in years past these wonderful women would
have been planning Thanksgiving dinner and baking pies
and creating a holiday to remember. This year, however,
they both cast a wary eye toward the day. "I'm trying to
be grateful," one said carefully. "I really am." I could hear
the guilt crouching behind her words, and it frustrated me
because I know her. I know she's not just *trying* to be grateful; she *is* grateful. She is thankful for her amazing children,
the beautiful marriage she shared with her husband for
thirty years, and for the way their core group of friends

surrounded them throughout his illness. She was deeply, dearly grateful, and yet, in the season of Thanksgiving, she felt that she wasn't thankful *enough*. What gives?

Here's my theory: we tend to expect gratitude to act as a sort of emotional acid, absorbing all sorrow on contact. Because of this underlying idea, we can also project that idea on those around us, and that's what had happened to my friend. The people who really, truly love her had run out of encouraging things to say and really wanted to enjoy Thanksgiving themselves, and so they resorted to advice like, "Just be grateful for what you *have*." And she was trying. And I am trying. And you are trying. But let's be clear: sorrow is not sin, and gratitude does not cancel out grief. Adoring her children does not eradicate the deep pain of losing her husband, and she needed—as we all need—permission to experience *both* joy and sorrow. When we stop viewing grief and gratitude as mutually exclusive emotions, we are well on our way to a healthier holiday, and I think Jesus told us this very thing in one little sentence that takes my breath away every time I read it:

> "Blessed are those who mourn, for they shall be comforted." (Matthew 5:4 NIV)

Bless. Mourn. Comfort. Three action words that seem at odds with one another at first glance but that, with a little synergy, form a strategy for enduring the happiest days in a season of heartache. A look at the original language shows us that we could lift the spiritually loaded word *blessed* up and out of that verse, drop in the word *happy,* and still be true to the meaning of the word. Happy are those who mourn? Ridiculous. It's like saying, "Healthy are those who are sick," or "Pregnant are those who are barren." This concept makes no sense until we add the third word: *comfort*.

Happy are those who mourn, for they shall be comforted.

Comfort is also a beautiful Greek word *parakaleo*. It's formed from two words: *kaleo*, which means "to call by name," and *para*, which means "near." This word pulls us right up into the lap of God and invites us to experience the beauty of His presence in a way we may never have experienced before. The comfort of God is a bigger, more powerful thing than we give it credit for being. It's in this uniquely "called by name" place that we are supernaturally strengthened, guided, and loved.

I recently took my husband to the hospital for surgery to have a feeding tube placed. Though we knew that ALS made him a high-risk patient, we were blindsided when the surgeon met us five minutes before the surgery and explained that his chances of coming out of the operating room on life support were very high and that we would then have to decide whether to continue that support or say good-bye. I'm not going to put a pretty face on this—we didn't handle it gracefully. We wept and shook and fell into a hug on his hospital bed as we tried to figure out which way to go. Without a feeding tube, his remaining days would be very, very difficult, and the longer we waited to have it done, the more risky it became. And yet—Steve had not said good-byes to our kids. Our son had left for school that morning having no idea that he might not talk to his dad again. Every option seemed impossible, and I felt like the walls were caving in on my heart.

This little event, though just a tiny glimpse at our story, represents the most difficult moment of my life so far. I've never felt such desperate sorrow. And yet (and I love this part), this event does not represent the worst moment of my life. The worst moments have been when I've wandered from God's plan or purpose, when I have not been able to feel Him in my pain. This deep-water morning, though, was filled to the brim with the *parakaleo* of God. I could almost hear Him whispering my name as I wept into my husband's neck. I could feel His arms closing in, just when I thought my heart would die inside my chest. And then we both heard His clear instruction to *wait*. At the same moment, we looked at each other and turned to the surgeon and said, "Not today." Comfort, love, guidance—it was all there in the middle of our sorrow because Jesus shows up when we suffer. He shows up, speaks our name, and reminds us it's okay to be broken with Him.

Finding Hidden Hope

Make two columns on a sheet of paper, labeling one *grief* and one *gratitude*. List all the things in each column, being brutally honest with how you're really feeling. Now write *blessed*, *mourn*, and *comfort* over the list, and ask Jesus to show you the ways He is working in every area of your life.

············

For strength, we thank You; it blesses us. For weakness, we thank You; it builds us. When all is bright, we thank You. In deepest dark, we trust You. And our souls sing It. Is. Well. Now, to the One who is able to do immeasurably more than we could ask or imagine, endless, eternal thanks.

Notes

1. Albert Barnes, "Isaiah chapter 9," *Notes on the Bible*, 1834, www.sacred-text.com/bib/barnes/isa009.htm.
2. *The Christbook*, vol 1 (Grand Rapids: Wm. B. Eerdmans), 24.
3. "Letter from John Adams to Abigail Adams, 3 July 1776, 'Had a Declaration . . .'" Adams Family Papers. Massachusetts Historical Society, retrieved June 28, 2009.